LAUNCH

LAUNCH

Let Your Setbacks Propel You Forward

Season Amber Burch

HAWAII WAY PUBLISHING
4118 West Harold Ct., Visalia, CA 93291
www.HAWAIIWAYPUBLISHING.com

For more information or to book an event contact HAWAII Way Publishing at HAWAIIWaypublishing@gmail.com, or 559-972-4168
Printed in the United States of America
ISBN 978-1-945384-21-9

TABLE OF CONTENTS

LAUNCH

Let Your Setbacks Propel You Forward
Season Amber Burch

My father spent his childhood in Wyoming, growing up on a large tract of land almost a mile from his nearest neighbor. When he wasn't in school, he spent his time working on the farm or running around the fields near his house. When he was quite young, without an adult present he wasn't allowed to carry a gun, but the one 'weapon' he and every kid he knew always carried with them was a wrist rocket – a slingshot that was either store-bought or homemade. He and his brothers all became crack shots with their slingshots. They would spend hours shooting cans and bottles off fence posts hundreds of feet away from them with amazing accuracy. When I turned 8 years old, my father passed this same skill on to me.

I was given my own wrist rocket and with his help, became very adept at knocking all of the cans off of our back fence at least a football field length away. My childhood wasn't that different from my father's. I grew up at the base of a mountain in a small western town. Running around barefoot, jumping off barns, riding bikes everywhere, climbing mountains and, of course, shooting a slingshot.

All the time that I was learning independence, I didn't realize how much I was learning about life. I remember so clearly carefully choosing the exact rock I needed for the direction I wanted it to fly. Pinching it securely between the worn leather at the end of my slingshot, pulling it back as far as I could stretch it, then carefully setting my sites on exactly where I wanted it to fly. Finally, I would release it and let it launch free.

Looking back, I realize now that I wasn't just learning to shoot a slingshot, I was learning how to concentrate, focus and breathe, so I could aim precisely and hit my goal. That was a great lesson I learned from the slingshot. Now that I have lived longer and endured more, I realize that I also learned so much from each of the rocks that I let fly. In life, we often feel like those stones. Whenever we are held back or feel stuck in place, we are really just preparing ourselves to launch. Resistance is the very thing that helps us fly.

One of our authors, Joe Koronowski, who was a NASA flight control officer for the International Space Station, has also taught me that force must be placed upon a rocket before it is able to take off. Bolts are set in place to stabilize it and hold it back. When the pressure has built up behind it enough that the rocket is finally able to push through all the forces working against it, the bolts explode, and the rocket is able to fly.

Like those launching that stone, or rocket, when great

forces seem to be working against us, that is the time that it's most important for us to concentrate on exactly where we want to go. It is often our difficulties that help us realize our purpose, correct our course and launch us exactly in the direction that we need to head. The authors in this book have been able to let their setbacks propel them forward and are here to teach you how you can do that too.

* * *

Season Amber Burch is an Author, Speaker, Publisher, Broker and a 'Cancer-Warrior Mama.' She has served as a National Spokesperson for St. Jude Children's Hospital for the past 10 years, and founded her own charity, Hats & Hair from Kids Who Care, which helps children facing life-threatening disease and hair loss. She is CEO of HAWAII Way Publishing, which stands for Health And Wealth And Inspired Ideas, and Editor & Chief of HAWAII Way Magazine. Her true passions are giving back, spreading hope, speaking to large audiences and helping others reach their goals, fulfill their dreams, and succeed. She also enjoys traveling with her husband and kids, connecting with fascinating people and teaching others to do the same. Watch for her soon to be released book, 28 DAYS TO HAPPY: A Healthy Abundant Positive Prosperous You! www.seasonamberburch.com

HOW TO REIGNITE YOUR PASSION WITHOUT BURNING OUT
Kerstin Moore, The Fire Coach

Do you live a life of passion? Do you experience joy and fulfillment on a regular basis? Or have you gotten stuck and forgotten what passion even looks like?

I believe that we are meant to live a life of joy and passion. Passion can be defined as "an intense desire or enthusiasm for something." Having passion is what motivates us to get out of bed. It's the fire that helps us wake up and say, "I'm so glad to be alive!" Passion doesn't necessarily have to be intense and all-consuming. In fact, prolonged, intense passion is not sustainable and will quickly lead to burnout.

Living a life with passion can be akin to living in a home with a constant gentle fire to keep the house warm. The fire gives you the light and warmth needed to properly do the activities needed for the day. With modern day convenience, we no longer need to light fires in our homes to be effective, but we still need to fan the flames inside our hearts. Living a life of passion can show up in many different ways:

5

- Having the energy to accomplish your tasks for the day and still have enough fuel to connect with loved ones in the evening.
- Finding joy in the simple things of life, such as enjoying the butterfly that crossed your path, or making your favorite meal for the day.
- Experiencing fulfilling connections with society as you go about your tasks.
- Having the motivation and drive to do your soul's purpose, whether that's creating an awesome line of code, making jewelry, gardening or organizing data.

So what is holding so many people back from living a life of passion and fulfillment? Passion can be diminished when we lose focus of what lit our fire to begin with. Have you ever seen a magnifying glass light a fire on dry paper? The magnifying glass harnesses all the power and energy from the sun and concentrates it into one small singular point. All the concentrated heat then starts the fire. If the concentrated point is too large, a fire cannot start. If there are multiple points from one magnifying glass, a fire cannot start.

What are some common reasons that we lose our focus?

1. We become over-burdened.

Perhaps there are too many tasks that we took on that don't fully honor our gifts and abilities. While these tasks may be important, they are distracting us from giving the majority of our energy to what is truly fulfilling and yields a return. This is similar to having multiple points in a magnifying glass and trying to start a fire.

2. We doubt ourselves.

Maybe there isn't an immediate return from living our passions and dreams. Perhaps we're afraid to take the first steps and instead choose hopelessness. Maybe we don't know what to do and are too afraid to seek answers. We then internalize the lack of immediate results, personalize the failure and then give up before the fire was lit, believing that we didn't have enough value to be spectacular. This is similar to holding the magnifying glass on the paper for five seconds, saying it'll never work and refusing to ask the teacher for help.

3. We need the passion to work.

We can identify when we are operating from a space of need when we are saying phrases like "I have to," "I must," "I should," "I need," "I ought to..." These phrases feel burdensome, constricting and controlling. Since when was passion burdensome?

When we are in a space of need, it is difficult to create what we want. We give our power away to external forces and rely on these forces for our happiness and fulfillment. When we are in a space of needing something to happen, we are not trusting the process and not opening ourselves up to receive. This is similar to having our heads hovering over the magnifying glass so the sun cannot get through to start the fire.

4. Attempting to live the wrong passion.

We may think we are passionate about something and put all our time and effort into that "passion," only to discover that truly isn't what we are passionate about. Perhaps we put all our efforts into the vehicle we are creating for our passion, so we assume we are passionate about the vehicle instead of the original passion itself. This is similar to attempting to light the concrete on fire instead of the dry paper.

There was a time where I was living a life of passion and then experienced extreme burnout. In 2010, I had just started a new career as a technical recruiter. My job was to help unemployed persons with computer-related skills find employment on a contract basis. Having previously experienced prolonged unemployment during the Great Recession of 2008, I was excited about the idea of helping others find a job that would work for them.

I got married that same year. I became a new wife and a mom to a curly-haired toddler. I was super passionate about creating a joyful life for my new son and building a happy family. I would regularly find activities for us to do on the weekends and would put extra effort into holidays. I had so much fun and joy in creating our new family life. I was the breadwinner, as my husband was finishing his engineering degree in school. Pretty soon, my passions dwindled as needs took over. My income was very much dependent on the commissions I received. While I found lots of joy and fulfillment in helping people find meaningful employment, I needed to hit certain numbers in order to provide for my family.

A year and a half after our wedding, I became pregnant with a darling little boy. I was so excited to be a birth mom and to finally have a baby. However, I needed more money to support my pregnant body, and the first year of having an infant can be quite expensive. The pressures upon me kept piling up until I couldn't take it anymore. A year after my son was born I had to quit my job, as I was diagnosed with stage 3 Adrenal Fatigue.

There were many factors that contributed to this illness. The bottom line is that I had such prolonged periods of stress and pressure that my body was overworked and had to start shutting down in order to survive. The first few months were incredibly difficult for me. If I tried to exercise, I would be bedridden for a week. I could get out of bed for an hour or two and then I'd be so fatigued that I had to get back in. I couldn't remember what I did the previous week, day or hour. I felt as if I was consigned to live a life of passionless misery. I finally had the baby I deeply wanted and was not in a space to fully enjoy him.

In those moments of darkness and bedridden despair, I realized I had a choice. I could accept my predicament and consign myself to a life of fatigue and sickness. I could throw my hands in the air, say, "Well, at least I tried" and create a negative belief that I don't deserve a life of passion and fulfillment. I tried once, it didn't work, so I might as well lie in bed for the rest of my life. That was a very real option for me, to give in to my health issues and let them dictate my life... OR I could choose to fight it. I could choose to accept my body as it was and work on what I could do to improve it. I could choose to live.

After 30+ years of life, I finally had the family relationships I had dreamed of, and I wasn't going to give it up because my body was shutting down. I chose to live and to reignite my passion. There were a few steps I intuitively followed to help reignite the passion in my life:

Step 1- Refocus on what you want

As I previously stated, the number one thing that causes us to lose our passion is when we lose our focus. When I first started working as a technical recruiter, I loved it because I was able to help and connect with people. I loved helping candidates find a job that fit their needs and provided a well-deserved income. Helping people brought me joy. As I previously stated, I lost sight of that passion because my focus became more on providing for the family and making sure I could make ends meet.

My focus was more on providing than on the things I truly enjoyed. Since the number one thing that held me back from living a life of passion, my job, was now gone I had to figure out what I really wanted in life. In order to refocus, I needed to take a sincere assessment of what I did and didn't like or want in my life, as well as what my strengths and weaknesses are. It's important to place your focus on what you do want and what your strengths are. When you focus your efforts on what you are good at, you feel confident about yourself and have the energy to keep doing what makes you feel good about yourself. The best way to create a sincere assessment is to make a list of the different areas of your life. Assess your job, your relationships, your finances and your health.

The first thing I assessed was my job. I took a deep look at what I liked about it and what I really didn't enjoy. I knew once I was done being sick, I wanted to go back to work, as being sick can be quite expensive. Instead of applying for any job, I was able to focus on what I really wanted in a job because I was able to figure out what wasn't working for me.

When it was time for me to go back to work, I was able to find a job that would create the most joy for me. From that job, I was able to discover that recruiting wasn't a true passion for me. It was more like an 8 out of 10. Once I was done with recruiting, I was done with peace and contentment because I had properly assessed my situation and kept refocusing on what I wanted.

However, during the year I spent in bed rest, it wasn't feasible for me to work. Instead of letting circumstance and sickness happen to me, I chose to focus on what I wanted: a healthy body. Creating a healthy body became an insatiable passion for me. Passion comes when we have purpose and drive. I had already decided that a full and complete recovery was possible, I just needed to figure out how.

I began to study adrenal fatigue, what it is, what causes it and how one can heal from it.

Adrenal fatigue is a form of weakness. I took time to understand how the weakness was showing up in my body: brain fog, weight gain, lethargy, overgrown candida, etc. Having a full assessment of the weaknesses in my body helped me focus on what needed to be healed. I then had to rely on my strengths to overcome these weaknesses. One of my natural strengths is that of research. As I mentioned previously, I researched all I could about adrenal fatigue. I read articles online, went to different doctors and asked questions on social media. Through this research, I created more clarity on what was going to work and what wasn't.

Another strength of mine is to create structure. In order to reclaim my health, I had to have some massive diet changes. Anyone who's done a major diet change knows that it's not the easiest or most fun thing to do. However, I found a lot of joy in looking up yummy recipes that fit within my dietary restrictions. I was able to create meal plans that made the new diet fun. Even better were the few diet appropriate treats I could make for me and the family.

As my focus was placed more on what I wanted, a healthy body, I was able to create more purpose and drive in my day. That doesn't mean my days weren't without challenges. There were many that I had to deal with. But I had focus and that focus helped reignite my fire for living my life.

2- Reconnect with what makes you happy

Once I started focusing on a purpose, to get healthy, it was time for me to reconnect with what made me happy. Because I had the wrong focus with my employment (making commissions so I could feed my family), I forgot what I enjoyed about it in the first place. What I really enjoyed about my job was connecting and helping people. I loved learning about the candidates, I would place on assignments and getting to know them on a more personal level.

I realized that connecting with people, and more importantly, my family is what brought me a lot of joy in life. More often than not, when we lose our passion, we tend to become disconnected and withdrawn from our loved ones. This doesn't mean you are depressed, although the symptoms may be similar. Going inward and becoming more isolated is a sure-fire way to smother the flames of passion. I truly believe that humans are interconnected and interdependent. We are social creatures and are divinely designed to need each other for success and well-being. Since human connection is what brings me the most joy, I did what I could with my limited capacities to connect to those around me and create fun experiences with the family.

I was able to find a discounted pass to a children's museum and would often take my children there for playtime. There were times I would go on walks with my children, once I had built up enough energy reserves, and I would chat with the neighbors.

I also refocused some of my attention back on to my adopted stepson. I got him into acting and would find some acting gigs for him. I spent time reconnecting him with his birth mom and her family, so he would know where he came from. Family history became an interest to me. I spent a lot of time doing the genealogy for my adopted stepson as well as my own. I found a lot of joy learning about my ancestors and the lives that they led, which helped me feel more connected to them.

Take the time to figure out what makes you truly happy. If money were no object, what would you do for the rest of your life? Allow your mind to expand to all the infinite possibilities and write them down without any judgment or excuses why it can't be possible. Out of the list, find the one that sticks out to you the most and find a way to do it. If dancing is a passion you always wanted to do but never could, find a place to learn how to dance and commit yourself to taking lessons. If that doesn't work, then allow yourself to dance while you do your daily activities.

If you've always wanted to travel but never felt you could afford it, take the time to look up how to travel cheaply. Then post pictures of the locations you want to travel so you can start getting excited about the future trips you will create. Remember, excitement is a vital aspect of creating your dreams.

What if you are already living your passion, but feel less excited by it? Chances are you've become so accustomed to living your dream that you forgot the excitement you once had about it. Take the time to remember what first got you fired up and excited about it. Remember how it felt to serve your first client and to see the success that came from your efforts. Or the enthusiasm you felt when you completed your first product and someone bought it. These are wins that motivate us to continue to move forward in the right direction. Even if you are so accustomed to winning it feels the same as buttering bread, take the time to actually enjoy the win and celebrate it like you won the Super Bowl! Who cares if someone thinks your celebration is silly? Small wins deserve to be celebrated just as much as the big wins.

Happiness is often rooted in the ability to tap into our creative abilities. We feel excited to see the magnificent things that we can create and it drives us to do more. Allow yourself to step into your creative abilities, whether that is organizing a closet, solving a technical problem, composing music, writing amazing sales copy, creating jewelry or fixing a leaky pipe.

Creativity isn't limited just to the artistic fields. It is connected to your ability to produce a desirable outcome. As I stated earlier, humans are designed to be interdependent. Don't be afraid to ask for help and support in living your passion. At times we get so bogged down in duties and responsibility that we put our passion last. What is burdensome to you is joyful for someone else. As you reach out and ask for support, you are creating a win-win situation. You get to live your passion and the person supporting you gets to live theirs. Never let money be an obstacle that holds you back from asking for help. There are always creative ways to establish an equal exchange of services rendered and received.

Set achievable, trackable goals

Our highest calling as human beings is to step into our own creative energies. At times this may feel daunting as we look toward a large opportunity in front of us. Being overwhelmed can cause us to lose focus and drive, which then causes us to lose our passion.

The best way to maintain your passion while creating is to set achievable, trackable goals.

Healing from adrenal fatigue is something that takes a long time. It isn't a quick, easy fix as I first thought it would be when I began my healing journey. When I first began, I felt that tracking my weight was a good way to track progress. I knew I had put on extra pounds because of the illness, so I believed that if I was able to track inches and pounds lost, I could feel successful in healing my body. I did the cleanses and diet changes recommended for healing my body from adrenal fatigue. I watched my body lose pounds and inches and felt very successful and positive in my results.

Eventually, the weight came back on out of no fault of my own and I felt like a failure. All that hard work and effort went down the drain. I would try the same tactics I used before, only to see that they weren't working. What I had to learn the hard way was that the extra weight was necessary in order for my body to fully heal and recover from this illness. In order for me to feel like a success and stay focused on moving forward, I found a different way to chart success.

To track my progress, I would compare the responses my body currently had versus old responses from the previous year. I could see how my body required fewer naps and could withstand greater physical activities. What used to wear me out and require several days of recovery, I could now do with ease and reduced downtime. For example, volunteering at three-day events would require several days, if not a week, of recovery time. Now, I may only need a day of extra sleeping in time after the event.

The two examples of goal tracking I shared can be put into two categories: tangible and intangible goals. Tangible goal tracking is what we typically think of when we track goals. It is easily quantified. One example of tangible goal tracking is marking things off of a to-do list. Another is measuring inches or pounds lost or the number of calls made. Or even charting progress by seeing how many words you have written for the day in the book you are writing.

Some ways of being successful with tangible goal tracking can include setting a timer for doing a certain task. That way your efforts are contained within a certain timeframe. You can remove all distractions and push hard for that time limit. Then when your time is up, you get to switch to something else.

I personally have a love/hate relationship with goal tracking. I love to feel accomplished, but I also don't like to feel boxed in. This is the solution I have created. I put all my worries and to-dos down on a list. Then I pick out the three most important ones and set forth to achieve them for that day. If the most important goal is to write a novel, I break it down into something achievable, such as write three sections of chapter 4 for the day. Remember, small wins add up to big wins. Often, I have noticed that my to-do list gets checked off faster than what I expect when I allow divine influences to guide my path. I find that what I thought would take forever didn't take as long as I expected.

There were times in the healing process where I would have a hormonal upheaval and couldn't be as productive as I'd like. I still set small, achievable goals to help me feel productive during the day. They may be as simple as:

1. Go to the gym
2. Do the dishes
3. Write that one blog post.

I may not have conquered the world, per se, but I still feel I achieved something, which helps keep the passion for life up and going. When it comes to intangible goals, I'm a big fan of those. These goals might be something like: Have greater peace in my life; Obtain a happier marriage; Gain a more positive outlook on my body. The truth is you can track these goals, you just need to know how.

The best way to track these kinds of goals is to take inventory of the attitudes and behaviors you would possess if you had already achieved your goal. Sometimes, it is helpful to inventory what you are currently doing that sabotages that result and set a goal to do the opposite. For example, if I had a goal to feel more socially accepted, the behavior that may sabotage this may be that I do not include myself in social gatherings and choose instead to be a wallflower. In order to achieve my goal of feeling more socially accepted, I would track how often I chose to speak up and include myself in conversations.

One idea for tracking these intangibles is to do a weekly check-in or progress report. Create a list of 5 to 10 behaviors or attitudes you would like to chart towards your intangible goal. Then rate how you feel you did on a scale of one to ten in that goal. You can write down why you feel you did well or why you feel there is room to improve. Over time you can see the numbers steadily climb up to show that you are achieving your intangible goal. For some, this is a system that can work very well. For others, it may be helpful to find a mentor who supports you in achieving your intangible goals, someone who is good at helping you see the progress that you may not see. The point of setting achievable, trackable goals is to show yourself how powerful you truly are. Success breeds success and helps you keep the fires of your passion burning.

So there you have it! The three simple steps to firing up your life: Refocus on what you want, reconnect to what makes you happy, and set achievable, trackable goals. These three simple steps can be used during any phase you are in.

They can help you avoid burnout and help rekindle your passion whenever you feel you have lost your spark. We all deserve to live a life full of passion, joy and fulfillment. Achieve that.

* * *

Kerstin Moore – Fire Coach, is dedicated to helping others rekindle the fire and passion within them. "Kerstin is as dynamic as she is intuitive and inspirational. Bold in her approach and masterful in technique, her program is LIFE CHANGING. If there is ANYTHING keeping you from the life you've always wanted then it's time to catapult yourself to the next level and that's what Kerstin does best. Kerstin has a finely-tuned radar when it comes to reading energy in people and wants to share her insight to help others." Originally from Texas, she studied at Brigham Young University and is President of More Empowered Inc. She is also working on her first book that will be out soon.

GRAND SLAM
Jennie Johnson

When I was young and life would throw me a curve ball, my dad would always sit me down for a talk. He was a former professional baseball player, so most of his advice included some kind of baseball analogy.

He would sit me down and say, "Sweetheart, the bases are loaded, there are two outs, two strikes, and three balls. What are you going to do? Are you going to strike out? Are you going to walk? Or are you going to hit a grand slam out of the park?

Even though I have heard this baseball analogy many times throughout my life, it always helped me dissect the problem and figure out how to handle it. The choice was mine. I could give up and strikeout. I could take an easier way out and walk. Or I could put all of my power into the problem and hit a grand slam to fix it. The solution to whatever problem I was facing was in my hands.

Only I could control the outcome of my life. But sometimes life throws you a curve ball that might just take you out of the game.

I had survived some pretty difficult times in my life, but I always seemed to come out of the situation stronger and a lot wiser than my years. I felt confident the rough times had passed and now I had everything I could have asked for. I was married to my soulmate, Doug. He was handsome, charismatic, funny, generous and worked really hard for our family. He kept life exciting. He never missed the chance to tease me -- or anyone else for that matter.

Our friends seemed to gravitate to our house. There was never a shortage of laughter that was usually at my expense. Doug loved to get a rise out of me. His humor was one of the reasons I fell in love with him. He had so many qualities that made him the man he was. He was the most generous man I had ever met. He always went out of his way to help others and had a soft spot for his elders. Doug worked in heating and air conditioning. He would often answer calls in the middle of the night and would never accept payment from his many elderly friends.

At that time, we had a 3-year-old baby boy named Travis, who was the apple of his daddy's eye. When Doug would come home from work, Travis would come running to his dad. Doug would pick him up and throw him in the air saying, "My boy, my boy!" Travis would giggle and wrap his arm around him and wouldn't leave his side the rest of the day. Whatever Doug did, Travis was determined to do with him. I would often watch Travis on his lap in the backhoe or on the 4-wheeler doing some project outside. When Doug was working in his garden, Travis was working right next to him.

All of our hopes and dreams seemed to be coming to fruition. I was pregnant with a baby girl who would complete our family. Doug had already named her, Brandi. We were in the middle of remodeling our home we had purchased two years' prior, that sat on one acre of land. My career had taken off as a real estate agent. Doug and I tried to work our schedule out so Travis rarely had a babysitter.

I came home from work one evening to find Doug and Travis covered in sheetrock dust. Travis's footprints covered all of our hardwood floors. I looked on in dismay at the mess I had to clean up. After watching them for a few minutes I couldn't help but laugh with them. Doug pulled me to the floor in my work clothes and made sure I was covered in white dust with them. This made Travis and Doug laugh even harder. Before long we were all covered in white dust and laughing.

I wanted to freeze time and enjoy the moment. In a few short months, Travis would no longer be the sole center of our attention. He was so excited to be a big brother, but I was uncertain how he would react to sharing our attention.

Over the next few months, I was full of anxiety. There was so much to get done before Brandi's arrival. On top of that stress, I had a terrible premonition that I was going to die. For some reason, I knew it wouldn't happen during childbirth. I can't explain why or what was going to take me away from my family. I was a healthy young woman, but the

25

feeling was so strong I couldn't ignore it. I tried to write it off as pregnancy hormones, but this nagging feeling didn't let up, so I started putting our affairs in order. I organized all of our paperwork, paid off every bill I could and prepared Doug to be a single father. I couldn't bring myself to tell Doug. I knew it sounded crazy and there was no need to worry him over a gut feeling.

I confided in a family member and my best friend. I made them promise to help Doug when the time came. I was certain they thought I had lost my mind, but they promised to help Doug *if* the time came. A few weeks later Doug came home with a gift-wrapped box. He told me how happy I made him and how much he loved me. I opened the box and tears came to my eyes. Inside the box was a beautiful sapphire ring. He had given me a special ring after Travis was born. He said "Thank you for doing everything for us and never thinking of yourself. Now you have a ring for Travis, one for Brandi, and one for me." He kissed my hand.

I wrapped my arms around him and gave him a kiss. I said, "I love you so much. How did I get so lucky?" I started to cry. I had everything I could dream of in that moment. I also felt panic. Everything was too perfect. I wanted to enjoy the moment, but I felt as if every special moment was leading up to the end for me. All I could do was take a deep breath to calm my anxiety and cherish the day. I was scared.

Doug had almost finished our remodel when Brandi was born. She was a few weeks early, but luckily perfectly healthy at 6 lbs. 13 oz. When the nurse was finished weighing her, Doug picked her up with so much pride. He was so caught up in the moment, everyone in the room faded away, including me. I said "Doug. Doug... hello! Can I see her?" He chuckled at himself as he handed *our daughter* to me.

Travis couldn't wait to hold his little sister when we arrived home from the hospital. He smiled big for the camera with Brandi in his arms. Much to my surprise, Travis was a natural big brother. Several days later, Doug turned 30 years old. We had a small party with the kids. Doug declared, "Brandi is the best gift you could have given me."

As the days and weeks went on, Doug came home for lunch every day to feed Brandi and take a quick nap with her. He wasn't able to do this with Travis, so I always had a bottle ready for him when he arrived home. There was a mellow contentment in our home. I was feeling less anxious about my nagging feeling. Maybe it was the pregnancy hormones.

Almost six weeks later, Mother's Day weekend had come. As usual, all of our family and friends gravitated to our house. Friday night we sat around the fire with close friends and family, and on Saturday we had a constant stream of people. We played horseshoes with a fun banter. Doug was known to be the life of the party and this day was no exception. He was happy. He draped his arm over his brother's shoulder. The two of them were on a mission to sweep the horseshoe game. It was soon decided we would all go out on a group date that night.

Doug bought me a new outfit and insisted I try it on for him. He arranged for his mom to watch the kids.

Early in the evening, Doug wanted to go home to put Brandi to bed. I wanted to join him, but he was adamant I stay and enjoy myself. Later, I came home to find Doug asleep in the recliner with Brandi in his arms and Travis on the couch clutching his stuffed animal.

As I put Travis and Brandi to bed, Doug woke up. He looked up at me with his beautiful blue eyes and whispered, "Thank you," as he pulled me onto his lap.

I ran my hand across his perfect, square jaw and asked him, "Thank you for what?" He looked at me with so much love, I knew he was feeling the same way I was. We had made it! All of the struggles of adjusting to married life, money, babies, jobs, etc. We had so much to be grateful for and so many things to look forward to, but tonight we had each other. He stood up and carried me to bed...

A few days later Brandi turned six weeks old. I was getting ready to go to my doctor's appointment. Travis was in the backyard playing while I was getting Brandi ready. As I turned to grab her diaper bag, to my surprise Doug was in the doorway watching us. He had an important meeting at work that morning, so I wasn't expecting him to be home.

His meeting was a success and he asked if I would mind if he went to the sand dunes to ride his motorcycle with his coworkers. I was happy he could have a day to himself. He had been working so hard at work, side jobs, remodeling our house and adjusting to having a new daughter.

He was concerned he would be missing my appointment. I was relieved because my nagging feeling was back, and I was certain I would find out what was wrong with me at this appointment. I had gone weeks without concern, but I had terrible anxiety that day. Doug looked me in the eyes and asked if I was okay. I wrapped my arms around him and gave him a kiss and told him, "I'm fine, go riding and enjoy yourself. You've worked so hard you could use a day off."
I watched out the front window as he drove away. I took a deep breath to calm my anxiety and went back to getting ready.

A few minutes later I heard Doug yell, "Goodbye, Jennie, I love you!" I picked up Brandi to see him and once again watched as he drove away. I sat at the window feeling even more anxious about my appointment. I was unsettled that Doug had turned around and come home just to tell me he loved me. I shook off my uneasy feeling and continued getting ready for the day to come. A few hours later, I carried a sleeping Travis into the house and went back to the car for Brandi. I was in high spirits. There was nothing wrong with me and my doctor declared I was perfectly healthy. I was so relieved. I couldn't wait for Doug to get home, so I could really enjoy our family without the constant worry that something bad was going to happen.

Later that day, several of our friends showed up to help Doug finish our remodel. I laughed at all of the jokes about his absence. Apparently, he forgot he had people coming over to help him. Before I knew it, it was 9:00 pm. Doug still wasn't home, so I decided to order pizza, knowing he would be starving when he got home. The kids and I were watching TV, waiting for Doug. Travis didn't want to go to bed until he saw his dad. I was holding Brandi when the phone rang. I was relieved because Doug was late.

I put Brandi down and ran to get the phone. I answered it with excitement and said, "Hey! Where are you?" I waited for his response but there wasn't one. "Doug, are you there?"

A voice on the other end said, "Jennie," in a cracked voice.

I said, "Hey Patrick, where are you guys?"

There was another pause. "Has the University of Utah Hospital called you?"

My stomach dropped. "What happened?!" Nothing but silence on the line. "Pat, what happened? Where's Doug?"

Pat stuttered, "Jennie, Doug is dead."

I heard a piercing scream. I thought, oh no, Brandi is crying. Wait, why am I on the grass? Doug's dead? No! No! The screaming was hurting my ears. What's happening? Why are my neighbors here? Oh no! Doug...

My neighbor picked me up and shook me. He asked, "What's wrong? Where's Doug?"

I was wailing and struggling to get away from him. I screamed, "Doug's dead!"

There are moments in life where you hit a brick wall and time stops. This was one of them. So many things were happening at once, yet I can't tell you a single detail, except for one. Travis. My sweet little Daddy's Boy. Oh no!

Everything stopped as I saw my sweet baby boy look at me with tears streaming down his face. He asked, "What does dead mean? Where's my daddy?"

I was scaring him. In that moment it dawned on me. When there is an accident, don't the police come to your door? If Doug was at the hospital maybe this was a big mistake. I had to hang on to hope, knowing Doug wouldn't give up on us. I wasn't about to give up on him. I took Travis in my arms and cuddled him. I told him I was going to go find out where his daddy was.

My neighbor helped me to the car to drive me to the hospital. The entire drive I prayed this was a mistake, but deep in my heart, I knew it wasn't. All of my anxiety over the past months finally made sense. But in that moment the thought was whisked away with pure grief, disbelief, fear, and so much more. All I could hear was, "Goodbye, Jennie, I love you!" Hearing his voice in my head helped me get to the hospital until it hit me, are those the last words I would ever hear from my husband? I wanted to freeze time and go back and tell him not to go riding. Oh God, what have I done?

"Goodbye, Jennie, I love you…"

We finally arrived at the hospital. I was out the door, running towards the Emergency Room before the car had come to a complete stop. I ran into the waiting room where his co-worker's wife stood up and said, "Jennie?" I shook my head. The only word I could get out of my mouth was, "Doug?"

She looked concerned and said, "Jennie, Doug isn't here."

My world went black. I don't know how long I had passed out. Long enough that I was taken to a private room with a trauma counselor and my neighbor.

I was informed Doug had already been turned over to the medical examiner's office for an autopsy. I couldn't see him until they released him to the funeral home.

All of this information was more than I could take. So many things didn't make any sense to me. I begged to see him, but they said it wasn't possible. I tried to argue with them, but Doug had never been taken to that hospital. It was out of their hands.

Over the next few days there was a constant stream of people, all wanting answers I didn't have. I tried calling the Sheriff's Department, but no one would return my calls. I had gone to the funeral home and made all of the arrangements for the funeral, but I still hadn't seen Doug. I couldn't completely accept his passing until I could see him.

The next morning the funeral home called to inform me I could see Doug. A few hours later I was led to a room where Doug was. Any hope I had that this was a mistake was taken away when I saw him. He looked so peaceful, so beautiful, but he was definitely gone. I couldn't believe this was how our story would end. We were supposed to grow old together. Raise our kids together. What was I going to do?

There was a shift in me after I saw Doug. First, I had to accept this nightmare was now my reality. Second, I felt Doug with me. Physically and spiritually with me. Time slowed down and I could breathe for the first time since I got there.

The next day was the funeral. I had gone back and forth whether Travis was old enough to go to the funeral. In the end, I decided he needed to understand what was happening and say goodbye to his dad.

We arrived at the funeral home early. I tried my best to explain to Travis what was happening but as soon as we walked in the room with Doug, Travis ran to the casket where I picked him up, so he could see his daddy. Travis said, "Daddy, daddy, wake up."

I tried to explain to him his daddy was in heaven. Travis heard his Grandpa in the hallway. He ran to him and yelled, "Gwampa, gwampa. I found my Daddy. He's asweep in a box." He was pulling his arm, so his Grandpa could see for himself.

The florist and employees from the funeral home all walked out of the room, crying. I was completely and utterly heartbroken. I brought Travis back into the room and explained to him his Daddy's spirit was in heaven. Travis tried to understand but at 3 years old he was appeased by finally finding his daddy.

The line for the viewing went all the way around the building. They estimated over 600 people were in attendance. I hadn't eaten since Wednesday morning; it was now Saturday afternoon. It was all I could do to stand next to his casket and thank people for coming. My dad stood behind me to keep me from passing out.

I couldn't believe the love and appreciation that was shown to Doug and our family. After hours of speaking with our friends and family and every other person Doug had an impact on, I was so proud to be his wife. I knew I had married the man of my dreams, but it's humbling to hear how many people Doug had touched. Whether it was his funny, cheerful personality or going above and beyond in his

34

daily life to help everyone around him, he had made a positive impact on so many people. The rest of the day was a blur laying Doug to rest.

A few days later the friends Doug had gone riding with came to the house. They were there to finally tell me what had happened that fateful day.

Doug died because everything that could go wrong, did. Everyone involved had failed to do their job, the BLM, the Sheriff's Department, his co-worker and the hospital for not dispatching life flight and not calling me. Doug passed away two and a half hours after the accident with two complete strangers by his side, waiting for help that never came.

I thought finding out what happened would help me come to terms with Doug's death. As it turned out, it left me with many more questions and I was angry that he was gone due to so many mistakes. He fought to stay with us, as I knew he would. The problem was, no one fought to help him. He was basically left for dead. The days turned into weeks while I isolated myself at home. The constant stream of people had slowed down. That was good in one way, but it left me with too much time to think. If it weren't for my kids needing me, I would have crawled into bed and stayed there.

In many ways, it was a blessing I had a 6-week-old baby to take care of. Brandi needed me every second of the day and Travis needed me to be his rock while he dealt with

35

the reality of his daddy being gone. I tried to hold myself together during the day but as soon as the kids were in bed, all of my emotions and fear came flooding out. I couldn't sleep in our bed without Doug so I moved Brandi's bassinet into the family room and slept on the couch with Travis.

After the funeral, Travis started having nightmares. He would wake up crying and reaching for his dad to come back to him. He would scream for his daddy not to leave him. He was so upset, it would take hours to get him back to sleep.

After a month of living in a completely isolated state, sleep deprivation and my inability to eat had begun to take its toll on me. My family was getting very worried and quite honestly, I was worried about myself too. I just didn't know what to do. I thought of my dad's advice. At that time, striking out felt like a pretty good option. I normally wasn't the type of person to let the hard knocks of life take me down. I needed to figure out how to get out of this depression and self-imposed isolation. Doug was never coming back and I needed to figure out how to accept it.

I can't explain why I had the feeling I would be the one to die. I realized by having that feeling, I unknowingly prepared myself to be a widow by putting all of our affairs in order. I had put myself in a more stable financial situation when I thought I was preparing Doug to be a single dad. Sometimes blessings are shown in unexplainable ways.

I needed to figure out how to get back to the land of the living. But how? I started by taking baby steps. Instead of falling apart after I put the kids to bed, I started writing down things I needed to do. At first, it was as simple as getting my hair done or taking Brandi back to the pediatrician, but it was a start. Over the next few weeks, I did a lot of soul-searching. I continued adding to my list, one item at a time. Every part of my life was different. The laughter that was a constant in our house was replaced by a sad silence.

I couldn't watch TV or listen to music. Every show we used to watch was now too hard to watch without Doug. Every song we used to listen to brought back too many memories. I needed to make a new normal for us. Somehow, I needed to bring back some of the happiness and laughter we were missing. I knew what Doug wanted for our family and how he wanted his kids to be raised. That knowledge helped me make promises to Doug. I never wanted my kids to grow up and say their life was ruined because their dad died. It was up to me to raise them in a happy, healthy home with laughter, love and security.

I started planning outings with the kids. We went to the zoo, the carnival, McDonald's Playland, the park, etc. I returned to planning play dates with other kids for Travis.

What used to be normal life was now a giant step forward for us. Keeping a routine was very important but it was exhausting. Every small step felt like I was running a marathon without my other half. Doug was gone but we were still alive. I needed to remind myself of that often and continue forward.

The days started to get a little easier, but I still dreaded the nighttime. That is when I missed Doug the most. One evening as I sat on the couch with Travis and held his hand, I got the chills as I looked at his hand in mine. It was Doug's hand. His unique square fingers were exactly like his dad's. I realized I may have lost Doug, but I still had a part of him. Our kids. So many of the things I loved about Doug were right in front of me. Every time Brandi looked at me, I saw Doug's deep blue eyes looking back. In a way, I would get to watch Doug grow up through our kids. That realization was the most comforting feeling I had since Doug passed.

I was feeling stronger each day. I started going back to our routine with the exception of all of the extra things I had to do now that it was just me. Doug had already planted his huge garden for the year. His family had been helping me a lot, but I needed to learn to do things on my own. With Brandi being a newborn, I knew I still needed the help, but I took over mowing our large yard. It was good exercise and helped me clear my head and stay centered.

Travis was getting back to his play work around the yard like he used to do with his dad. Now he did it with me. He was turning into a little man. He would say things like,

"Don't worry, Mom, when I grow up I'll build you a new house." Or "Mom, I'll get a job when I grow up and buy you a new car." As cute as these statements were, I realized he was taking the comment "you're the man of the house" too serious. No one meant harm by saying that, but Travis had taken the statement literally. Some things can't be undone but I needed to show him I was strong enough for all of us.

My small steps forward started to get bigger. I started cooking again. I made a point to set the table with my china every Sunday. It was usually just for me, Travis and Brandi in her high chair, but it brought back a sense of normalcy in our life. I also figured out a way to continue the work that needed to get done on the house. Instead of doing it for our enjoyment, I knew I needed to sell the house to downsize. I had a lot to do before it would be ready to sell and I needed to be creative to raise enough money to do it. I started selling everything we no longer needed. The hardest item to sell was the motorcycle, yet it was also the item I wanted to get rid of the fastest.

My first project was our bedroom. I knew I needed to move back into our room to create normalcy for all of us. I hadn't let anyone touch our room. Everything was the exact same as the day Doug died. I was starting with the hardest project. I realize now it was the right room to start with. At the time, it was excruciating to pack up all of Doug's clothes. I could smell Doug the second I entered the room. As comforting as that was, I knew I needed to take this step forward. Doug's mom had a great idea. She took all of Doug's favorite shirts and made two quilts out of them for the kids. Before long, our room was transformed into my room. I purposely made it very feminine for a complete change. As I was doing projects at home, I started taking time for myself without the kids. Each time I left the house, I started feeling like a woman instead of only identifying myself as a mom or a widow. I made time to go to the salon, tanning or go to lunch with friends. This routine became vital to my survival as a single mom. I had to become an individual person again.

I made an effort to get ready each day. I still hadn't gone back to work. It was very easy to stay in yoga pants and Doug's t-shirts every day. I needed to feel good about myself and that included taking the time to get dressed, put makeup on and do my hair. It sounds simple, but it wasn't. I didn't have anyone coming home to see me at the end of the day. This was for my own self-esteem. Part of getting my strength back as a self-confident woman was taking the time and energy to feel good about myself, just for me.

Of course, I couldn't just think of myself. Every decision I made included the promises I made to Doug to do what was best for Travis and Brandi, not just what was best for myself. Each day I was feeling much stronger. Less like a victim and more like a single mom trying to navigate a world full of changes. With each change, I learned something new about myself and found a strength I never thought I was capable of. I know I made my share of mistakes. It's impossible to navigate any difficult life path and get everything right. Looking back, I think the mistakes taught me the most and made me the strongest.

Before I knew it, Brandi had turned one year old and we had made it to the first anniversary of Doug's death. This date meant we had made it through an entire year of "firsts." Every holiday, anniversary, birthday, etc., was a huge accomplishment for all three of us. Every first without Doug was so hard. Many were spent at the cemetery where Travis and Brandi sent balloons to their dad in heaven. We had a barbeque that day to celebrate Doug's life, the way he would want us to. Not at the cemetery, but at our house with family and friends. Our house was once again full of laughter, telling stories about Doug. I knew Doug's memory would always stay alive through his children and our memories of a man who made an impact on so many people's lives. People that will always help Travis and Brandi remember who their dad was.

Three years later, I received a phone call from my dad. He said, "Hi, Sweetheart, how are you doing?"

I said, "We're doing good, Dad. I'm still getting our new house in order. Travis loves his 1st grade teacher and Brandi just started preschool this week."

My dad cleared his throat and said, "Sweetheart, I'm proud of you. You hit your grand slam." My dad went on to tell me how proud he was of me and how well I had handled Doug's death. For forty-five minutes he told me everything I ever hoped or dreamed I would hear from my dad. I hung up the phone and sat in awe, realizing we had made it. I had my dad's verdict that I hit a grand slam. Amazing!

Later that night my Dad died of a heart attack.

As I drove myself to the hospital to meet my mom it felt like deja vu. I prayed for my Mom. I also thanked the Lord for the many blessings I had received. I had been blessed to receive the gift of my husband's last words that helped me survive the hardest days of my life.

As I drove I replayed my conversation with my dad that morning and knew I had once again been blessed with my dad's last words to me and knew they would help me be strong enough to get through this loss.

As I parked my car at the hospital, I was preparing myself to be strong enough to help my mom go through the same journey I had just survived. I was full of gratitude that the two most important men in my life left this world with the gift of *their* words. I can't think of a better blessing to be left with.

"Goodbye, Jennie, I love you!" and "Sweetheart, I'm proud of you. You hit your grand slam."

***

Jennie Johnson continues to use her dad's advice to help navigate life challenges. She has kept every promise she made to her husband after his death. Her children have thrived and were raised to feel blessed in the knowledge their dad would always watch over them. Life continued to throw curve balls her way, but she has tried to embrace the difficult times, knowing there is always a life lesson in the making. She lives in Utah where she continues to practice Real Estate.

JOY BEYOND LIFE'S TRIALS AND TRAUMAS
Annadel Lemon

I remember so many wonderful things from when I was a kid. We didn't really stay inside much, we were always out looking for adventure. We moved a lot because it seemed that my dad was always starting a new farming job every few years. We would spend most of our summer days swimming in various bodies of water. There was even a pond near one of our homes on the farm my dad was working at. The crazy thing is that it seemed my sister, who is 4 years older than me, and my brother, who was 2 years younger, and I were often at the pond alone. I was only about 4 at the time. My parents would take us to the lake too; Black Sands Resort. For most families this would be family time. My mom would swim with us sometimes, but usually, she and Dad would be drinking at the bar while we swam.

Another fun memory is my brother and I playing Cowboys and Indians outside and using the big round propane tank as a horse. My sister would sneak into the outside freezer where my mom hid the Christmas goodies and get us all something to eat (she mainly shared so she would have an accomplice). One year Mom sewed most of our Christmas gifts; blankets for our dolls, clothes for our Barbies, and clothes for us. She was an amazing seamstress. That same Christmas we snuck into the gifts to open them before Christmas. Mom knew what we did and warned us that it would ruin Christmas morning. She was right.

I also remember that my dad was never sober unless I saw him in the morning before he left for work, which was hardly ever. He was a functional drunk, though, and waited until he was not working to start drinking. I don't remember any of us ever having a great relationship with him, either. Kind of like he lived there but he was not at all present.

However, I choose to remember the fun memories and not dwell on the trauma that was a huge part of my childhood existence. If someone else would have been dropped into my life they would have been in shock, and wonder how this life was real. To me it was just my life.

There were things in my childhood that were quite traumatic, leading up to the major trauma my sister, brother and I faced. Things like when my parents would leave my 8-year-old sister to babysit 4-year-old me and my 2-year-old brother while they went out to the bar. Things like leaving us in a freezing cold car in December in Eastern Idaho, while they stopped at their favorite bar on the way to Grandma's for Christmas.

Then there was the time when my dad purposely pulled on the steering wheel of the car while my mom was driving and ran the car off the road. Another time when I was very young my dad came home looking for my mom, who must have gone out without him. He came to get his shotgun to hunt her down. This situation was abated only by my grandmother (his mom) who was living with us at the time as we cared for my dying grandfather.

These severe volatile situations seemed to lessen as I got older but the drinking never did. Despite some of the bad parenting decisions my mom made, she loved us and I was close to her. I never felt like we were neglected by her emotionally or physically. She was a fun mom and very loving to our friends too.

The night that set my life on a path that I will never forget was December 30, 1982. I had a best friend who was more of a sister to me than just a friend. We would spend one week at my house and one week at her house. We were inseparable. I decided that I was going to spend the night with her that night because my sister was going to town and I could get a ride. As we were leaving I saw my mom standing at the screen door, waving. I thought about how cute she was and wanted to go back and give her a hug, but my sister was in a hurry to leave, so I thought I would just hug her when we got back.

My friend and I were having a fun time just hanging out and we decided to do the new Jane Fonda Workout tape. (Some of you younger readers will have to Google it.) As we were following along with Jane in her leg warmers and French-cut leotard, there was a knock at the door. We thought this was strange because it was now about 10:00 at night.

When we answered the door, there was a police officer standing there and he wanted to talk to me. He had me sit down and proceeded to tell me that my mother had been shot and had not survived. They were looking for my father as the main suspect in her murder and we were to stay away from the windows because he was considered armed and dangerous.

My friend's mom took me to the hospital where I met up with my brother and sister. The next morning, we were told that my dad had been found. He had parked his truck behind his friend's house, hooked a hose up to the exhaust, ran it into the cab of his truck and left the truck running. There I was, age 15, my brother, age 13, and we were without parents because of a selfish and traumatic act of another. My sister was 19 and married so she was able to take us in. Your life can change in an instant and you never know how you will deal with trauma when it hits you. But I can tell you that you always have a choice. You can choose to let it destroy you, or you can choose to push through and become stronger than you were before. You can choose to be a victim or a victor.

I chose to be a victor and to become stronger and help others through their own traumas. You may not be facing this big of a tragedy, or yours may be much bigger. Either way, I have some steps that I used in my own journey and some other tools I learned along the way that I want to share with you to help you step into your best self.

Gratitude: If you are experiencing fresh trauma or tragedy you may be thinking, "Are you kidding me, you want me to be grateful for my situation?" You would be 100% justified in asking this question. Who in their right mind would be able to have gratitude at such a hard time in their life?

When I lost my mom I did not feel grateful for that situation. I didn't think it was fair and I was mad that I had been left without my mom. Eventually you will be able to actively think about things you are grateful for, but first, you need to allow yourself to feel the pain and grief of the experience.
Many times when you live in a highly religious society like I do, we put extra pressure on ourselves and allow guilt to overtake us for not feeling gratitude. Never allow guilt to creep in while you are in the grief process because you are unable to feel grateful for your situation.

A few years after the loss of my parents I was on a date and he asked me how I was able to deal with the loss of my parents and seem so okay. I realized at that moment that I had learned to develop gratitude for my situation. At the time of my parents' deaths, my life was not going in a great direction. I was dating a guy that was not good for me. My parents didn't care if I drank and so I did, many times while they were there because they were busy drinking themselves.

After the tragedy in my life, I found my religion and was in a much better place spiritually. Looking back after even more years, I am able to see how blessed I am because of the turn my life took at that very traumatic moment. Many times the farther removed we are from the incident, the more blessings we can see.

There isn't a set timeframe for you to be able to feel gratitude. It is individual to each person. Just do not allow yourself to stay stuck too long. Three ways you can begin to find gratitude are:

1. Write a list of 100 things you are thankful for. In order to help you with this list, use the guideline I use. What if everything I didn't thank God for today was gone tomorrow? These are the things I put on my list. When I think about it that way, it becomes easy to write my list.

2. Keep a Gratitude Journal. At the end of the day write at least 3 things you are grateful for that day. If you are having a really bad day and can't think of anything, refer to your master list. Doing this will make you more aware of the people, situations and things in your daily life that you are glad are there.

3. Call, text, or email someone in your life and tell them why you are grateful for them. Not only does it make you look for people in your life you are grateful for but it also makes you think a bit about why you care about them. This will help strengthen relationships, which you need while going through the healing process.

Forgiveness: For many years I did not forgive my father for his actions. I held bitterness in my heart that was very deep. I had moved past it but had not really dealt with it. By most accounts, I had every right to hold on to the bitterness. Why should I give him forgiveness after his actions? He left three children without parents. I would have had every right not to.

However, even if I felt he did not deserve forgiveness, I needed it for myself. I needed to be relieved of the bitter heart I had been carrying. At first, I did a token forgiveness of just letting it go. This did take some time, because as I talked about in step

1, you need to allow yourself the time that is needed to get through these processes.

Indira Gandhi said, "Forgiveness is a virtue of the brave." I wanted to hold on to it because I had not felt brave enough to deal with it. This is the reason full and true forgiveness is obtained in steps or phases; we get braver with time and practice.

My first step was to just let it go and not really think about it. I felt I had moved on so I must have forgiven to an extent. It wasn't until I was studying my energy healing modality that I realized I had a block that was holding me back from my full potential in learning and experiencing the techniques I was being taught.

That night before my class I really took a look at where these blocks were. I realized that not only did I need to really forgive my father, but I had a block with my mother as well. I needed to get to the bottom of the emotions that were blocking me. I decided to use a technique I learned for one of my mentors that I call *finishing the conversation*.

Most people who have endured trauma know who the person or people are that have been the sources of their pain. So start there with having the conversation. If possible, find a tree. The tree will serve as the person you need to finish the conversation with. Yes, you are going to talk to the tree.

The reason I suggest the tree is because as a living thing, the energy will be more similar to that of speaking to a human. (I have also done this just in my car, so if you don't have the ability to be alone by a tree, any quiet, secluded place will do.) Ask the tree if it is okay that it stands in for the person you want to finish the conversation with. (Hint: the tree always says yes.)

To begin the conversation, ask the person if you can speak to them. Remember, you are not talking directly to the person; you are speaking to the tree as them or just their spirit. This conversation needs to be very intense. Get everything out that you have ever wanted to say. I usually recommend swearing and yelling, if that's what it takes. Tell them all the reasons they have caused you hurt, pain and trauma. Once you have really dug deep into the emotions around this person and the events that caused the trauma, you will feel a huge release.

The next step is the most important and the most difficult. After you have released all of the negative emotions on the person, it is now time to tell them you forgive them and to ask them to forgive you for having the bad feelings toward them.

Yes, you ask their forgiveness. This does not mean that what they did to you was okay. When people hurt you it is never okay, but you can have a forgiving heart. Remember, this is more for you than them.

When we do not forgive someone who has wronged us it creates a negative energy connection with them. Imagine in your mind what static on a radio might look like. The negative energy created is like that and it has a powerful effect in holding us to the person in a negative way with that "static." Forgiveness releases you from that static field and sets you free.

One thing I did when having this conversation with my father was to meet him where he was at. I had to understand where he was coming from and try to think about why he would do such a thing. While not excusing it, I wanted to put some understanding into it.

After yelling and telling him how horrible I thought he was, I said, "I'm going to meet you where you are at and try to understand that the amount of alcohol you consumed caused brain damage of sorts. I understand you were not in your right mind. This doesn't mean what you did was okay, but I understand you were not of sound mind." Meeting someone where they are at is very helpful in allowing yourself to forgive them.

For me, the next level of forgiveness came through a friend of mine. He was very intuitive but didn't really know he was. We were at an event and we had both left the meeting to use the restroom. When we met in the hall we started talking. Prior to this, I had just had an experience that helped me see that I needed a deeper release of the emotions around my parents' deaths. We talked about this for a bit and he just stopped and said, "Your father had something terrible happen to him when he was a young boy that caused him to try to do whatever it took to erase it. It wasn't his fault."

By being open to receive this information, I was able to get this gift from my friend and accept an even deeper forgiveness of my father. If this information had been presented to me early on I would have never accepted it. Enough time had passed for me and enough work had been done on my part to be brave enough to forgive even deeper.

Take back your power: In the book *"Power vs. Force"* by David R. Hawkins, the author discusses the vibrational frequency of emotions. Using muscle testing, he developed a chart showing how weak or strong the emotions we feel are, ranging from 20 to 1000.

When we experience emotional trauma, the emotions we feel vibrate at the lowest level. These include shame, guilt, grief, fear and anger, with shame vibrating at just 20, which is near death. This is why those who have had trauma, especially in childhood, have a 12 times higher rate of suicide than those who have not dealt with trauma in their lives.

When we have gone through trauma we often feel victimized. When we feel like a victim we are experiencing many of these lower vibrational emotions. Just because you have been a victim of trauma does not mean you have to stay there. Never use your circumstances as an excuse to stay stuck. Living as a victim will never allow you to move forward in life and find your true success and happiness.

Taking back my power and becoming a victor instead of a victim was the most critical thing I did to start myself on the healing journey. It did not matter what my father did to cause me pain. I decided I would no longer allow it to make me feel shame about who my father was, or feel sad and angry.

I chose to raise my vibration, and you can too. Empower yourself and do not let others who may have hurt you in the past hold your power. Say out loud, as often as necessary, "I am taking back my power and I will no longer live as a victim. Today I choose to step into my greatness!" This is a great phrase to use during your *finishing the conversation* too. No one can make you feel anything. You choose to allow it. Choose to stand fully in your power and you will see a huge shift in your success and happiness.

As I made my way and still make my way through these steps, I become much more kind and understanding. I have learned to think about what someone may be going through to cause their actions. I try to be more patient even in traffic when someone cuts me off. I try not to judge others.

I am not perfect at these things but I continue to strive to be better than I was yesterday. I have been so blessed using these steps and I can say that I have true joy and happiness in my life.

Honor your past. It has made you who you are today. Have gratitude for the present, for that is where you live. And look to the future with hope, since that is where you are heading.

***

Annadel Lemon, "The Freedom Warrior," is the owner of Freedom Warrior Wellness in Bountiful, Utah. She is a Mentor, Keynote Speaker, Certified Energy Practitioner and Health Coach. Annadel is an expert at helping free people from negative emotional trauma so they can clearly see their potential and step into greatness. She uses tried-and-true mentoring techniques, and lessons learned along her own trauma journey to mentor others to success in business, health, and relationships. She has been featured on the California TV show "Spotlight: The Allison H. Larson Show," as well as "The Spotlight Radio Show" and numerous other radio and podcast appearances. Annadel is the author of the upcoming book, "Beyond the Pie Hole: 7 Steps to Shedding Your Emotional and Physical Fat Suit." She currently has two audio CDs, "Trauma Mamas: Self Care for Adoptive Parents of Hard Kids," and "Brain Scrub: Cleaning Out Negative Thoughts to Make Room for the Good Stuff." Annadel is also a member of The Speakers Coalition and Speak Up. She is a wife to her wonderful husband, Lester, and is the mother of 6 children: 3 by birth and 3 through adoption; plus stepmom to 3 young men.

NOTHING WILL STOP ME
Mikayla Tea

My biggest setback in life happened when I was only
12 years old. I was a competitive cheerleader who loved to
win at everything I did. Whether it was cooking dinner or
playing a board game, I loved to have fun and compete. I was
young, naïve and didn't really care that much about anything
other than school and family. I thought everything was a
game. I didn't really have any responsibilities, other than
school, work and chores. I wasn't all that mature and alert. I
was just like the average sixth-grade girl trying to survive
middle school.

I was at school on a Tuesday afternoon as I walked in
to my fifth period art class. I wasn't feeling good, I couldn't
breathe, I was hot, dehydrated and I really had to go the
bathroom (though I had gone just a few minutes before).

My teachers had been asking me if I felt okay
throughout the past few weeks. I thought they were just
hallucinating or something. One of my teachers said that I
looked skinnier and asked if I had been losing weight. I
responded, "I don't know, I just started cheerleading, so
possibly." She said that wasn't a good thing and I just
laughed and walked away. Another teacher also told me that

I looked pale like a ghost, but I blew her off as I ran to hang out with friends.

But that day when I walked into class I actually *felt* like I was dying. I instantly told the teacher that I did not feel good. She had been questioning me for weeks. She looked at me and sent me to the nurse immediately. I ran into one of my teachers on the way. She asked what I was doing and I told her I was going to the nurse. She questioned me about several things, like if and what I was eating. She said I looked anorexic. I was too dizzy to understand what she meant so I pushed on to the nurse's office.

When I arrived at the nurse's office she let me lay down, gave me water and took my temperature. She then got this panicked look on her face and called the counselor, principal and the two assistant principals. I had fallen asleep and woke up when they all came in. I was scared and embarrassed to see them all there staring at me.

The principal started asking me what I ate for lunch. I told her everything that I had eaten for lunch, for dinner the day before, for breakfast and for every meal I had recently. Everyone there said they thought I was anorexic because I was really skinny and really pale. I was scared. I was only 12 years old and didn't know what that meant or was happening.

My mom showed up at the nurse's office what seemed like a few minutes later and I could see the fear in her eyes.

She kept whispering something to herself and looking away but grabbed me close and made me feel better as she helped carry me out to the car to go home. My mom told me later that I looked like a skeleton. She said you could see every bone in my body and I was incredibly pale.

My mom thought I was losing weight due to working out too much and lack of protein, so she made me a protein shake. She then let me lay on the couch and I fell asleep wrapped up in blankets. I was finally warm. I woke up about every two hours for around two minutes at a time, and fell back into a very deep sleep.

Eventually, my mom woke me up and gave me some soup, but I didn't feel like eating. Then she told me she had a meeting to go to, but she could cancel it if I needed her to. I told her I knew that we needed the money, so she needed to go to her meeting.

Mom left for her meeting very worried about me and made several calls asking people to come stay with me. My brother was at church and I was alone at home and I just laid on the couch and kept sleeping. My mom told me if I needed anything to call my dad or my grandma. My parents are divorced and my dad was still at work.

I was scared so I called my grandma and she came over and brought me fruit popsicles, saying they made her feel better when she was sick. Being a 12-year-old who liked sugar, I happily ate a popsicle.

My grandma did not want to get sick and she had to work early the next morning, so she left. I started to feel worse and ended up calling my dad to see if he would come over to stay with me or take me to the hospital. He told me that he was tired and he wanted to go home and relax because he just worked eight hours. I was alone and I fell asleep again.

I woke up and I think my mom and brother were carrying me up the stairs. I wasn't really sure because I fell back asleep. I was dizzy and felt like I was on laughing gas at the dentist's office. They had to carry me because my mom tried to wake me up several times but was unable to. They took me to my mom's room.

My mom later told me she thought I was going to die, that's why they took me to her room. When my brother set me down he said, "Sis, I can feel every bone in your body." My mom shushed him with a weird look as tears ran down her face. We argued when I asked her why she was crying and all she said was she just had a hard day. She whispered to my brother to go call 911.

My mom held me in her arms while she waited for the paramedics to come. She later told me she was holding me in her arms because she said if I was going to die she wanted me to die in her arms. Lucky for me, I survived, and each day is a new gift that I am so very grateful for.

The next time I woke up I was in my mom's bed. I could hear my brother on the phone, he was yelling, "She's not well, we've called the paramedics. We're going to the hospital. We are scared that she could die."

I heard the front door open and voices downstairs, then footsteps following her upstairs. I was scared, so I jumped up and went to the hallway as my mom and the group of medical people rounded the corner to come help me. I yelled, "No, mom, I'm fine. I'm fine. Tell them to go away." I had never been to the hospital since the day I was born. I had never broken a bone and had never been sick other than the common cold. I was certainly not about to ruin that perfect record.

I was terrified. I didn't know was happening and all I saw was paramedics with these big scary machines and sharp needles coming my way. My mom told me to lay down on the bed again. They said they were going to check my blood sugar. My blood sugar was 469 (an average blood sugar should be anywhere from 80 to 180). I didn't understand what this meant.

They paramedics ended up taking me to the hospital and admitting me. I was scared. They stuck an IV in my arm and all I remember seeing was the clock and the ceiling of the hospital room. The hospital nurses were very worried about me and kept pulling my mom and dad out of the room to talk.

Around 4:00 A.M. they put me in an ambulance and transferred me to the children's Intensive Care Unit down the road. I don't remember what happened the first few days, I was asleep for most of it. I remember them telling me I had Type One Diabetes and all I thought was, *okay, well, can you just give me the medicine and let me go home now*?

Little did I know that every day for the rest of my life I would be taking a minimum of six shots a day. I didn't understand the struggles I was going to need to get through. I didn't understand what it meant. I didn't understand how I got it. I thought it was like a cold, you take some medicine and it goes away.

I remember when they drew blood out of my arm it felt cold and limp. I hadn't eaten in two days, but I remembered food and asked when I could have some, but they said I had to wait. My family came in from California and all over town. I didn't understand why they were all there. I thought I was just sick with a cold or the flu. I saw my mom and my dad crying and my brother getting angry and sad.

Half a week into my hospital stay a lady came in to teach me about diabetes. They brought in food wrappers to teach me about nutrition labels and how to count carbs and how to equate them to my shots. They brought in needles and a piece of fruit for us to practice giving shots. They explained to me what happened.

63

My understanding of what happened to me was my insulin-producing enzymes that are in my pancreas were killed by something in my body, because my body mistook my pancreas for a germ or something that was harming me. One person explained that my body killed my pancreas (whatever that was).

The doctor came in later and gave me a shot, let me eat and then told me that every day for the rest of my life I was going to have to take a shot every time I eat and a couple more each day. They said the good news was I could still eat whatever I wanted and didn't need to change what I eat. They even told me for my first meal I could have French Toast!

They taught me about high and low blood sugar and also how to manage my diabetes by the amount of insulin I take in each shot. They said my family and friends had to learn to give me my shots. I had to give myself shots before I could be released from the hospital.

They had me walk around the hospital. I got lightheaded a lot because I'd been in the hospital bed for almost two weeks. I was finally released and went home. I spent another two weeks at home before I went back to school.

Going back to school I noticed a lot of things I never noticed before. There were three other diabetics at my school. We all had to go to the nurse's office early, and we had a great nurse.

A lot of things changed around me. Diabetes has made my life more difficult but in many ways it has also made my life better. It has given me my own story to tell and a cause to champion in my life.

What I have learned through all of this is that everything in life happens for a reason. We may not always like that reason but it's what was intended for us. Through the whole process of finding out that I was a diabetic, I had to look for the positives to stay upbeat. Every day is a gift and it is not to be taken for granted.

What helped me through all this was praying, the love and support from my family and true friends. From that point on I have the permanent job of acting like I am my own pancreas. There are no shortcuts to take because the second I take a shortcut my life is on the line. The same goes for everything else in life. Shortcuts are for the quitters who are not willing to put in the effort to succeed.

When things get rough for me, whether it's diabetes or just things in life, I talk to my mom, or go to YouTube and I turn on motivational speeches. The motivational speeches help me to persevere through whatever is going on in my life at that moment.

What overcoming my fear taught me was you have to step outside of your comfort zone. It is outside your comfort zone where success becomes a reality.

I never let diabetes hold me back from achieving my dreams. As a matter of fact, I don't let anyone, or anything get in the way of me achieving my goals. I am a dream chaser who knows whatever I work and strive for, I can achieve. Because of what I have been through, I am mature beyond my years. I'm also a fighter for what I believe in because I have had to learn to rely on myself and know how strong I really am.

My success in my life has been realized from overcoming and learning to live with diabetes. I have diabetes to thank for helping me overcome one of my biggest fears: my fear of needles. Believe it or not, I was deathly afraid of needles when I was young. Now I take many shots a day and prick my fingers almost as often.

I am making it through all of this not because of A, B or C, I am making it because of me. I push myself through all of this by using the help of others around me to stay strong, expressing my emotions, leaning on those who love and support me, and getting hugs when I need it most.

It's important for us all to reach out and get the love and support that we need as well as learning that you already have the strength that you need in you to power through.

***

Mikayla Tea is a 14-year-old author, entrepreneur, professional speaker, actor, anti-bullying and healthy community advocate, Youth City Council Member, Champion of her life as a Type 1 Diabetic and incredible achiever. She is also an award-winning athlete/competitive cheerleader, businesswoman, overcomer, fighter & life preserver. She is an incredible young woman who constantly strives for her goals and is certain to succeed.

OVERCOMING THE FEAR OF LOSS

Marie White

When we write about ourselves it is easy to say what we do for a living, where we live or even what we enjoy. But whenever I meet a new person every fiber of my being wants to say, "Hello. My name is Marie and I am the parent of an abducted child." An event like that defines who you are. Not that the event happened, but how you choose to continue each day will define you.

Since that horrible day, I have become a YouTube host, a non-denominational Christian missionary and the award-winning, bestselling author of five books. I could say, "Hello, my name is Marie and I am a writer." But this book isn't about saying what I am, but who I am. And who I am is a hurting mom who wakes up every day thinking about our missing child and praying for the day our child comes home. When our child was abducted I had a choice to make. I could say, "Lord, you did this and I hate you." Or I could stretch my gaze beyond the horizon and look for the end result to this tragedy.

After all, if God had allowed it, then there had to be a reason. And so began my three year journey turning over every stone, looking for the final piece of the puzzle. I felt that once I completed the puzzle, our child would come home. My search has led me to the tops of volcanoes in Hawaii, the rugged mountains of Colorado, through the Arches of Utah, across the Mojave Desert and into the hearts and homes of over half a million viewers around the world.

In my quest I've ridden horses, whitewater rafted, kayaked on the ocean, hiked mountains, flown in a helicopter and been on too many planes to count.

My life feels like the end of the movie *Titanic,* where you see all the adventures the woman has gone on, but the whole time there was a hole in her heart that no breathtaking sunrise could fill.

Growing up I always wanted to be an actress and world-traveler. I starred in my own reality show for years before reality shows existed. My show was in my mind and the audience loved it. As we are living we are discovering who we are. Does the joy of your childhood lemonade stand mean you're an entrepreneur? Your love for animals surely destines you to be a vet, right? Facing the school bully made you aware of defending the defenseless. But here we are, in phase two of life and it's a new beginning. A reawakening of discovering who we were always meant to be.

What about those things we regret? The lost loves, the lost chances. Did you forgo the chance to backpack Europe due to a passing love interest? What about the business chances you should have taken, but hesitated too long and lost the opportunity?

Now you've learned to take chances and seize the day. One of the things that go through a setback does is give you the opportunity to reassess your goals. What are your personal goals? Professional goals? Financial goals?

If you've hit rock bottom and landed on your backside, then the view before you is the dirt. But the view above you is the sky. Just turn around and keep looking up. It's about coming into your own. There are certain things that you can't be regarded as an expert in until you've put in your 10,000 hours. No one wants to hear a 20-year-old talk about the proper way to be a grandparent. We want someone with extensive experience or overwhelming success at a particular thing. That expertise takes time. This second half of life is ripe with opportunities to use the knowledge and experience you've attained and probably didn't even know you had.

Once I was talking to a young man who was discussing how his Christian faith was affecting him in his college classes. His classmates sometimes turned their noses at answers to the professor that pointed to his faith. As he described the distance he felt from some of the other students I was able to encourage him with something that was a known fact to me. But because of his youth and inexperience, to him, it was a revelation. I said, "You know that these are the same classmates who will come to you when their parents get divorced, they wind up pregnant, their grandmother dies, or they are feeling hopeless. On a dark night, one of them will come up to you and ask you to pray for them or invite you to tell them how you handle these types of events. Unknowingly they are cataloging you in their minds as someone they can turn to."

His face lit up. He had never known this or even thought of it. I had experienced it for years and heard about it weekly from friends and family members or read it in articles. My 10,000+ hours as a Christian had made me an expert in parts of it, and to this, I could attest with complete confidence.

What are you an expert in?

Author Malcolm Gladwell talks about the 10,000 hour rule in his book *Outliers*. The gist of it is that to be among the best at something you have to have 10,000 hours of "deliberate practice." For me, the bottom line is that our child is not home yet. I don't know when they will be and sometimes I despair that they will not come home at all, but not entirely. The other day I received an email from a missionary friend in Greece who wrote me to say that during her prayer time she had been praying for us and that God had pressed upon her heart that our child would come home. It was a reminder of what I already knew, our child will be home soon and God is still working toward this. For now, I concentrate on writing books, marketing and connecting with people.

Meanwhile, we wait.

In the book *Failing Forward* by John Maxwell, it says, "Failures see failure as an all-encompassing event and Successes see it as a one-time event." My personality is more apt to say, "Hey, I did that wrong. What can I learn from it?" While other personality types may say, "I'm a mess-up and I'm no good."

Some days I think that life will continue on without our child, and I will make it if I have to. Other days I'm not sure that I can handle another minute without the smell of my sweet baby's hair as I hold them close to me.

My question is always, "How much longer, Lord?"

Legolas, in *The Lord of the Rings,* said, "They run as if the very whips of their masters were behind them." I too feel an urgent push to get as many things accomplished as I can before our child comes home.

When something bad happens we all have some pretty standard responses. We can feel:

Abandoned

Angry

Dazed

In despair

Empty

Afraid

Guilty

Jealous

Nervous

Numb

Stressed

One of the comments made about my fifth book, *Strength for Parents of Missing Children: Surviving Divorce, Abduction, Runaways and Foster Care* was that it wasn't just for parents of missing kids. Everyone who read it found it to be an uplifting book about overcoming tragedy. Who knew? I thought that I was writing to parents who were going through what we were going through and instead I found that people everywhere were reading it for inspiration.

The obstacle that you are trying to overcome may just be the stepping-off point for something far bigger than you could imagine. As you read in this book about cancer patients turned victors and wayward youths who become successes on Wall Street and others finding their life's mission and pursuing their dreams, you will continue to see that what has pulled you down is also what propels you forward.

One of my favorite movies is *The Princess Bride.* Everyone knows that movie. Let's look at Wesley's story. In the movie, Wesley falls in love with the daughter of his wealthy employer. An extremely poor farmhand, Wesley leaves to make his fortune so that he can marry the woman he loves. But once Wesley leaves the farm he is captured by the deadliest pirate of the seas, Dread Pirate Roberts. Wesley is attacked, held prisoner and told each day that he will be murdered.

In this moment Wesley has a choice to make and it's the same choice that you and I have. Will Wesley choose to be broken by this twist of fate -- alone, captive, threatened daily with death, and kept from his one true love? In his eyes, his life was over. Everything he had ever hoped for was gone. He had no promise of living through the next day and definitely no chance at making it back to his true love.

Wesley could have become bitter, hating the pirates who had taken his freedom, cursing God for this harsh end to his dreams and leaning into his despair. Instead, Wesley chose neither to become broken nor bitter. He chose to become better. Wesley became a better person. He pleaded with his captor for another chance to live, he trained and fixed his eyes on the horizon. He held in his mind the hope that one day he would make it back to the woman he loved. And guess what? His reality far exceeded his dreams.

Instead of making enough money to marry the girl he loved, he became the Dread Pirate Roberts himself. Using his captive time to learn a new skill as he became a master swordsman, an intellect and a decisive strategist, he would return to his true love as a legend. Not only did he get the girl, but he would, in fact, save her from being murdered. He would thwart the plot by an evil king to send the country into an unnecessary war and rid the land of many wicked people.

His beginnings were humble, his goal was noble, but because of his hardship, his story's end would be beyond his wildest imagination, and so can yours. While Wesley's story is fiction, it is based on scores of stories from history where we see person after person who were each faced with the same type of situation. Look at Esther, who was taken captive and became queen, or Joseph, who was sold as a slave by his brothers and became second in command over all of Egypt.

Esther could have despaired early in her journey. Her parents were killed when she was a child; that would be enough to destroy anyone, but still, she persevered. She was raised by a loving and godly uncle who regarded her as his own daughter. But even that safety was taken away when her beauty made her a target for the king's harem. Being a young Hebrew woman, taken into the harem of a pagan king had to shake her to the core. How could she live according to God's commandments? What had she done to deserve this? Then Esther is chosen to become the queen over Babylon. What an honor. But it also meant there was no going home.

However, God's plan for Esther had not been revealed yet. It would turn out that Esther was placed on that throne for the precise moment when all of the Jewish people would be targeted for annihilation by a wicked and evil man. For

Esther to speak to the king about this could cost her life. She was going to be silent until her uncle sent her a message, "For if you remain silent at this time, relief and deliverance for the Jews will arise from another place, but you and your father's family will perish. And who knows but that you have come to your royal position for such a time as this?" (Esther 4:14.)

In the Christian community, we use this phrase often, "For such a time as this." It's a shortened version of the verse above. It reminds us that God places us in certain situations for a reason and that we are there at a divinely appointed time. You are reading this now because this is the time that was appointed for you to read it. There is something that God wants to tell you that you could only hear at this perfect time. What is it?

With my missionary work, I talk to people around the globe who are choosing to follow God as Christians, at great peril to themselves. For many people, making the choice to become a true Christian means leaving their current religion. The cost is very high. Here in the US that may mean losing all your friends, your family, your business and your identity. What would it cost you to walk away from your current religion or way of life? Would you choose to change your current religion if you found absolute truth? Sadly, many people won't. They will go to their deathbeds with these words on their lips, "I knew the truth but thought the cost was too high. I missed the truth and the cost has been high."

What if I had dug in my heels? What if I had said, "God, you did this to me. You obviously don't care and I'm not going to listen to you ever again." I've touched the lives of over a million people. Messages come in weekly from countries around the globe about how my YouTube channel, books or missionary work has impacted their lives.

What if I had said no?

What if I had refused this terrible privilege?

Would my child still be missing? Yes. Would my heart still be in pain? Yes. But there would be one less missionary. Five fewer books. A million less lives touched by the love of Christ.

Joseph had this same choice to make. He was a teenager when his jealous older brothers sold him to some passing merchants. What would an act like that do to your self-esteem? God had already given him prophetic dreams revealing that he would be the head of his family, now here he was, at the bottom of a dry well while his brothers bartered over the price they would sell him for.

Joseph could have become bitter about his own family turning against him. Instead, he chose to be the best slave he could be to the man who bought him in Egypt. Through his good attitude, trustworthiness and God's divine plan, he was promoted to the head of his master's household. Then, when all was going well, his master's wife tried to sleep with him. Joseph was a very handsome young man and the wife kept at it. I'm sure that it was tempting for Joseph, if even just for a moment. What did he have to lose? He had nothing, and as a young man his hormones would have been raging. The only real possession that Joseph had was his master's trust and his trust in God. That was enough.

The Bible says: So Potiphar left everything he had in Joseph's care; with Joseph in charge, he did not concern himself with anything except the food he ate. Now Joseph was well-built and handsome, and after a while, his master's wife took notice of Joseph and said, "Come to bed with me!" But he refused. "With me in charge," he told her, "my master does not concern himself with anything in the house; everything he owns he has entrusted to my care. No one is greater in this house than I am. My master has withheld nothing from me except you because you are his wife. How then could I do such a wicked thing and sin against God?" And though she spoke to Joseph day after day, he refused to go to bed with her or even be with her. (Genesis 39:6-10)

As many of us have seen, justice doesn't always come in the way that we think it should. Joseph's brothers weren't scorched by a bolt of lightning for their evil deeds, and as we will see, Joseph wasn't given justice either. Even after Joseph decided not to sleep with his master's wife, she kept pursuing him. Finally, he ran away from her and in her anger, she grabbed his cloak, screaming that he had attacked her. Joseph ended up in the royal prison for a crime he didn't commit.

Again, Joseph could have become bitter, but he chose to be the best version of himself and ended up running the prison. His story could have ended there, but it didn't. In prison, Joseph meets two of the pharaoh's advisors who promise to mention him to Pharaoh. Instead one of them dies and the other forgets about him. But when the day comes that the Pharaoh needs a dream interpreter, the advisor remembers the man he met in prison years before. This is the final act in Joseph's three-act play. He begins as a naïve boy with grand visions, ends up in slavery and prison, and the story reaches a climax as he interprets the pharaoh's dream and rules over the most powerful nation.

The Pharaoh makes Joseph the grand vizier (second-in-command) over all of Egypt. He gives Joseph the daughter of a powerful man as his wife and Joseph saves Egypt from the annihilation of a severe famine that spreads across the entire region. Eventually, Joseph's own family travels down to Egypt in search of food and he is reunited in a reunion that only God could orchestrate. Joseph tells his brothers that what they intended for evil, God intended for good. The pages of this book are filled with stories just like that. People who have been through the worst that life has to offer and instead of being broken or bitter, they have chosen to be better. You can choose that too.

Given the choice, I'm sure that Joseph would have wanted to stay with his family and have an idyllic childhood. The path God had for him was fraught with injustice and heartache, but in the end, each event prepared him for a future that only God could see and a destiny far beyond his wildest dreams.

That's our challenge, isn't it? We want a life that's uneventful and filled with good things, but growth doesn't come from our peaceful moments. It's in our hardest battles that we find out just how weak or strong we are. It seems odd, but the same moment can show us where our weaknesses lie. I know that for me when I'm in physical pain I'm more easily discouraged. Being sick or injured makes my defenses weak. But in the midst of devastating loss, I found that I was far stronger than I ever thought I could be. What have your challenges shown you?

In *When God Doesn't Make Sense*, Dr. James Dobson wrote, "the majority of us will someday feel alienated from God. Why? Because those who live long enough will eventually be confronted by happenings they will not understand. That is the human condition. Let me say it again: It is an incorrect view of scripture to say that we will always comprehend what God is doing and how our suffering and disappointment fit into His plan. Sooner or later, most of us will come to a point where it appears that God has lost control-or interest-in the affairs of people. It is only an illusion, but one with dangerous implications for spiritual and mental health. Interestingly enough, pain and suffering do not cause the greatest damage. Confusion is the factor that shreds one's faith."

Sometimes we are tempted to make rash decisions just to get past the stress of having to make a decision about our goals in life. In his book *Winning with Integrity*, Leigh Steinberg said that cognitive dissonance "suggests that the psyche can tolerate only so much indecision and wavering between the poles of a difficult choice. At a certain point, the strained psyche forces the conflicted person to make a decision simply to relieve the tension and anxiety. Unfortunately, this relief is short-lived, and the person then finds himself often facing the larger challenge and greater confusion of living with or working his way out of a bad move -- a choice of the wrong career; a purchase of the wrong automobile; a marriage to the wrong person."

During my childhood, my family moved about every two years. At first I lamented the fact that I had to start a new school for the coming school year. But after several towns, I began to see the benefits of moving. Mistakes I'd made, like getting my shirt stuck in my zipper in the third grade, did not have to travel with me. No one knew about the boy I had a crush on and who found me invisible. The day I ran crying from the playground was long forgotten. Each new town was a fresh start. Yes, I missed my friends and the familiarity of the last town, but new things can be exotic, even if they are just dirt roads in small farm towns.

These experiences taught me about new beginnings and how to see the good in difficult situations. Some people move and never get past the loss. Others run wildly into the newness. I try to run with abandon toward new things, even if they frighten me. I don't want to get stuck by being afraid of change. What would you do if you had the chance to pack up and move to a new place? Where would you go? Who would you hope to meet?

Would you be a writer, sipping coffee in a villa in the south of France, golden sunsets glowing off the coast? Would you trek the wilds of the jungle in Brazil, sleeping beneath a sea of stars that look close enough to touch? How about hiking Mount Kilimanjaro or Everest? Do either of those cause adrenaline to race through your body? What excites you? What makes you want to be the best version of yourself?

I spoke at an event by a non-profit for families who have been separated from their children. In my speech, I asked the audience to make a choice to become the best version of themselves. When we go to court or church or an important meeting we don't go in our grubby painting clothes. No, we wear our Sunday best. No one at the meeting thinks that on weekends we wear business suits and ties. It's not being disingenuous. It is about putting our best foot forward, being the best version of ourselves.

There are some families and religions that force their members to pretend to be better versions of themselves than they are. That is disingenuous. Putting on your Sunday best is different than that. I am asking you to look at who you are inside and put on the outside the best of what you have to offer. If you're a caring person, then choose to care. If you're a talker, then talk. If you're a listener, then listen.

When we go through hard times it's easy to pull ourselves into our shells, like a turtle who is afraid to come out. Instead, we need to be defiant of the hard things and tackle them with gusto. It's easier said than done, but if I can do it, so can you. You were wonderfully and beautifully created to be the best version of yourself.

* * *

Marie White (www.MarieWhiteAuthor.com) is the author of six books, including the award-winning, #1 bestseller, Strength for Parents of Missing Children: Surviving Divorce, Abduction, Runaways and Foster Care. She is also a missionary, traveler and YouTube host of Bible Stories for Adults. She encourages people from all walks of life and experiencing a variety of struggles, to know that God is on your side.

FROM FRACTURED TO REMISSION

Gina Estrada

Imagine you received a call from your spouse telling you to pack a bag because he is on the way to pick you up and take you to the emergency room. Doctor's orders...

On Friday, May 20, 2016, I stepped off a curb while carrying a heavy piece of art my husband and I had just purchased from an estate sale. I remember this day clearly because it was exactly one week after my husband, Bob, had a heart attack in the middle of the night and was whisked away in an ambulance. It had been his second heart attack in six months. It was a very scary time.

Luckily, Bob had awesome doctors and is doing fine now. Okay, if you must know, the art piece I was carrying was part of "The Sopranos" television series memorabilia... his choice. Since Bob was fresh out of the hospital he wasn't supposed to do any heavy lifting. Being the healthy one in the family, I had no problem lifting the large, heavy piece and carrying it to the car.

As I approached the car at the end of the walkway I didn't realize I was at the curb until I flew off it, causing my hips, ribs, and back to take a jolting impact. Fortunately, I didn't fall and I didn't drop the piece of art, which was covered with a heavy piece of glass. I ended up in major pain, it hurt to breathe. I had fractured ribs.

I have been somewhat accident prone my whole life. Let's just say I have had a few trips to the emergency room for broken bones, stitches in my head, stitches in my hand... you get the picture. I didn't think too much of fractured ribs because there isn't a lot you can do for ribs except wait for them to heal. Normally, I healed quickly. I had no reason to believe this time would be any different. Oh... but it was. By July 2016, I was in a great deal of pain. I wasn't feeling any better. I wasn't healing. My primary care physician sent me to physical therapy. It didn't help.

In August 2016, my friend, a local oncologist, Dr. Christopher Perkins, was visiting our home. He noticed I was in major pain and suggested I get an MRI. Over the next week, I had an MRI, a bone biopsy, and a PET scan followed by a blood test.

On September 6, 2016, Dr. Perkins called my husband and told him to take me to the ER immediately. It is funny now, that when I received the call from Bob telling me to pack a bag because I was going to the emergency room, I didn't even question why, or for how long. I quickly grabbed my backpack, threw in a pair of underwear, a toothbrush and toothpaste, hairbrush, face wash, cell phone, iPad, and chargers. By this time my body was in so much pain I could barely walk. In fact, I was already using a walker to get around.

On my way to the hospital, I recall thinking that at least I would get the answers to why I was in so much pain and get the help I needed to relieve it. What happened upon my arrival was not exactly what I was expecting. As I was admitted, Dr. Perkins diagnosed me with Stage 3 Multiple Myeloma Cancer (there are only 3 stages), told me my organs were shutting down, my bones were fractured due to my cancer tumors and to get my affairs in order.

Unlike not questioning why I needed to pack a bag, I had a plethora of questions running through my brain. What the heck is Multiple Myeloma? (Multiple Myeloma is cancer of the plasma cells. Plasma cells are found mainly in bone marrow, the soft substance inside some hollow bones where blood cells are produced. Plasma cells are an important part of the body's immune system. Symptoms include bone pain, fractures, anemia, and lower resistance to infection.) How did I get it? What can I do to get rid of it? Am I really going to die now? Do I have a fighting chance? Where are my kids? I've been meaning to clean out my pantry for months now, it's a bit disorganized... how embarrassing. Get my affairs in order... like right now, or do I have a week or two? Am I going to die here in the hospital? I've lived a great life, if it is my time, I am at peace and I want others to be at peace too, I think? When do I get another dose of painkillers? Little did I know I would spend the next 45 days in bed in excruciating pain. I couldn't even roll over or lift my arms. I literally had fractures all over my upper body and pelvis. It was truly a time of chaos and confusion.

How do you develop or maintain a healing mindset during a time when your life has been turned upside down or a time of hopelessness? My simple -- or not so simple -- answer is, you have to train your brain. First, we will define a healing mindset as a fixed mental attitude or disposition that predetermines a person's responses to their interpretations of situations. It refers to habits of mind formed by previous experience, an intention, or inclination.

How do you approach "bad news" when you get it? Do you give up, exaggerate, reach out to others for help, run for cover, hide, or go into denial? I believe mindset is the most important part of the healing journey.

My story is about Multiple Myeloma Cancer. However, I believe you can interchange the word "cancer" with any other tragedy one might encounter such as divorce, death, disability, bankruptcy, rape, diagnosis of disease, abduction, or any other highly stressful situation.

For this chapter, I will use the word "cancer" to mean any tragic, life-altering situation. Here I will share with you the steps I took on a daily basis to maintain and further develop my healing mindset. And if followed, you can too, no matter what you or a loved one might be going through at this time. I want you to know that you are not alone. There are people who have gone through or are going through what you are experiencing at this time and there is help. You must be willing to ask for it.

If you are anything like me, asking for help is an extremely hard lesson to learn. I was always the one providing help to others, not asking for help. Read on to discover what I learned when I had to reach out for help. I believe the following three steps are necessary if we are to develop or maintain a healing mindset during a time of chaos and confusion. I will share with you how to pull them all together and put them into practice on a daily basis.

STEP ONE: Take "IT" on fully. Once the cancer was identified in my body and I accepted the fact I could die from it, my body and mind seemed to be at peace; I calmed down. It is the resistance to things that keep us stuck. At the time I had to move on to how I was going to get rid of my cancer and the pain. One of Tony Robbins' great quotes that resonated with me is, "Identify your problems, but give your power and energy to the solution." I decided to give all my power and energy to the solution. It didn't matter why or how I got cancer, I wanted to focus on healing and getting rid of it as soon as possible. Whatever you may be going through at this time, can you accept it? Can you decide right now to take it on fully? Once you have accepted the "cancer," you are free to give your power and energy to the solution.

STEP TWO: Have FAITH. "Faith without absolute Positive Belief is Dead" --Napoleon Hill. No one says it's going to be easy. I will never say this whole process was easy because it was the hardest thing I have ever had to go through. I can't imagine anything harder than having to fight for your own life at a time when you are at the weakest point of your life, bedridden and experiencing excruciating pain because your body is fractured.

If your body is operating at a high-stress level at all times, it cannot heal. The Bible teaches us over 365 times to have faith and not fear. We cannot live in a state of fear and faith at the same time; we must choose. I chose faith, which was much easier than living in fear. Courage is not the absence of fear, but the presence of faith. The Bible teaches us in Joshua 1:9 (NIV), "Have I not commanded you? Be strong and courageous. Do not be afraid; do not be discouraged, for the Lord your God will be with you wherever you go."

In the Book of Joy, by Douglas Abrams, the Dalai Lama, and Archbishop Desmond Tutu, the Dalai Lama answered the question regarding how it is possible to experience joy even at times of suffering and adversity. He shared, "There is a Tibetan saying that adversities can turn into good opportunities. Even a tragic situation can become an opportunity. There's another Tibetan saying that it is actually the painful experiences that shine the light on the nature of happiness. They do this by bringing joyful experiences into sharp relief." I hope you will give some time and energy to living in faith and not fear. The choice is yours.

STEP THREE: Remain PRESENT. About nine years ago I took a beginning meditation class. I love learning something new. What I didn't know was how valuable the meditation lessons I learned would become in my life. In the beginning of practicing meditation, I remember struggling to focus on quieting my mind, focusing on my breath for only one to three minutes, but with practice and training, it became much easier.

There are many books written on the subject of remaining present and meditation, as well as numerous YouTube videos you can check out. Here is a quick overview of how to get yourself in a state of remaining present quickly: close your eyes, take a deep breath, focus on your breathing. You don't have to worry about what happened in the past or what you think might happen in the future. All you have to do is focus on the present. This can be done during any stressful situation or at a time when you feel chaos looming around you. It is human nature to get all wound up, caught up in the chaos and confusion. Choosing to remain present is done by interrupting the pattern. You can consciously choose to remain in the moment. You can choose to be proactive rather than reactive.

I remember sitting in the church during the Celebration of Life for my Aunt Sarah. She died tragically when she hit her head on a curb after the driver of the golf cart she was standing on took a sharp turn and she flew off the cart. She was a member of the Blackhawk Chorus in Blackhawk, California. The chorus was singing beautiful songs at her ceremony. I was overtaken with emotion. Tears were running down my face, at times I felt I couldn't breathe. In the middle of the tears, I reminded myself to breathe and remain present, so I could remember and celebrate my aunt's life. I closed my eyes, focused on my breath for a few moments, and I was able to focus on the words of the songs, the singer's faces, and the family and friends around me. I was then able to take it all in.

Again, it takes the training of your brain to be able to pull it all together during a time of extreme emotion. I am thankful I had the knowledge and training on how to remain present, so I could form the beautiful memories I now carry with me from her Celebration of Life ceremony.

You may be asking yourself, why is remaining present so important? It is really what ties Step One and Steps Two together. Either Step One or Two cannot be accomplished without remaining present. A great time to practice is when you aren't in the middle of a crisis.

Early on in the diagnosis of Multiple Myeloma, I was overwhelmed with the outpouring of love and support from my family, close friends and my community. Choosing to remain present led me to develop deeper relationships with all those coming to my bedside. It was an awesome experience.

I remember conscientiously asking myself with each visit, why is this person here with me now, beyond the fact they were visiting me because I was sick and in the hospital. By going beyond the "why" they were there and the "why" they chose to show up at my bedside, I was able to find a way to actually give back to them in some manner, even though I was bedridden and not able to move.

You can try this today with all the people you come in contact with. It is super easy to get in the state of mind: 1. Close your eyes. 2. Take a deep breath in and let it out slowly. 3. Over the next few breaths, ask yourself, "why is this person here with me now?" (Think beyond the initial reason.) 4. Start your interactions with the person focusing on the present moment, carefully listening to their words, followed by asking good questions to figure out the "why." The other person doesn't have to know what you are doing, you can do it peacefully and quietly "behind the scenes." I used my business/networking skills, beginning with what I can give to others first, not what I can get. This is the approach I chose to begin my healing journey.

"Whatever you're thinking, think bigger." -- Tony Heish, CEO of Zappos.

Okay, Gina, this is all great information, but how do I put it into practice on a daily basis? I'm so glad you asked... here is a simple six-step process that can be completed in as little as ten minutes or as long as two hours. It is up to you to make it work for you in the allotted time you have.

I suggest if you are in the middle of chaos and confusion, take the two hours for yourself. Dedicate two hours per day to work on YOU. Why not? You are worth it! If it means you have to get up an hour earlier, DO IT! If it means you have to let your significant others know this is your time, DO IT! If it feels a little selfish, it's not. We all need to take the time to get into the right mindset before we go about our day.

"Before everything else, getting ready is the secret of success." -- Henry Ford

In July of 2015, my book club read the book, "The Miracle Morning," by Hal Elrod. In the book, he challenges his readers to take the 30-day challenge of what Hal calls "the SAVERS." Each letter in SAVERS stands for a step in the Miracle Morning process. After the 30-day challenge with the book club, I experienced so many positive results I continued practicing my Miracle Morning and have done so every morning since. When one wakes up each morning with purpose, the possibilities are endless.

There are many famous people who have a morning routine they follow. What they all have in common is they do it every single day, no matter what -- it's a priority. In this chapter, I share my morning routine and how I remained positive and maintained a healing mindset in the midst of chaos and confusion because I committed to waking up each day with purpose and practice. My morning routine created a space for me to "put" cancer where I could identify it, but focus my power and energy on healing.

Prayer & Meditation: The first thing I do every morning is wake up and ask myself, what am I grateful for this morning? The first morning I woke up in the hospital I was grateful for being alive and I was grateful for the pain relief I was receiving. My process is once I decide what I'm grateful for at the moment, I pray. After that, I take a little time to sit in silence.

Whether you pray or meditate or haven't done either in the past, the important thing is to get started. The main thing is to stay positive first thing in the morning. This will train your brain to focus on the positive and let the negative "stuff" go. It seems strange to be thankful for "cancer," but being thankful for the diagnosis gave me relief, helped me accept it and resolve to move forward from there. During my recovery, I included praying for others as part of my morning silence.

Visually Create a Plan: Proverbs 29:19, "Where there is no vision, the people perish, but he that keeps the law, happy is he." The body follows what we visualize. It doesn't discern what is real and what is imagined. Depending on the day, I visualize everything about making the next day better than the last, being able to stand up and deliver a speech, lift my arms, play golf again, etc.

Visualization is part of creating a plan. This step also keeps your mind focused on positive things. I didn't think about the fact I couldn't get out of bed or even roll over in bed, I focused on what I wanted. I really wanted to be able to walk again without pain. Rather than worrying about what I couldn't do, I visualized doing the things I really wanted to do with all my might. Vision keeps what you want at the forefront. You have a choice. We need to stay awake and not just live life on autopilot, like a robot.

"Gratitude makes sense of our past, brings peace for today, and creates a vision for tomorrow." -- Melody Beattie

Exercise: As a former aerobics instructor for 15 years, I love to exercise. Whether you love to exercise or not, I recommend 30 minutes daily. What you choose to do is up to you. What do you like to do? I recommend keeping it simple, choosing something that is easy and something you enjoy. I recommend beginning with a 30-minute walk, especially if you are in a time of crises. Don't stress your body more by putting it through rigorous exercise.

When I was in bed for 45 days, obviously I couldn't take a walk, but I did things in bed that led to me being able to eventually walk again. In the beginning, I could point and flex my feet and hands. Eventually, I could slide my feet towards my buttocks and back down. Whatever I could do, I would do it every day.

Whatever you can do at this time, do it each day. Even if you can't make it 30 minutes, just get started doing something you can do on a daily basis. You will be training your brain and body to be strong. Your body will begin to crave the movement.

"Don't wait, do it now. Don't wait until you are ready to take action." -- Jim Rohn

Reading & Writing: Spending a little time in the morning by reading something uplifting is again, training your brain to remain positive. Since I am in a book club, I read the assigned chapters for our next book club discussion. This step is totally up to you. Well, I guess all the steps are totally up to you, but this one has a wide range of possibilities.

An easy place to start is to pick up a daily motivational or devotional type book and commit to reading it each morning. I like to read a devotional type book with room to journal each day so the next year I can look back at each day's notes and see how far I have grown.

Establishing a daily devotional practice will promote self-discipline, shaping us and correcting things about ourselves that we need to change in order to heal and move forward in our life. It will help increase your faith and give you hope.

"Reading is to the mind what exercise is to the body." -- Joseph Addison

You can choose to write about anything you wish. In the beginning of my morning routine, I chose to write a blog on a topic of Business Networking. When I got sick I changed my writing to more of a diary type so I could get all that "stuff" out of my head.

When you write something down, you don't have to think about it again unless you really want to. The journaling gave me another place to "put" the pain.

I approached my writing with "Today is going to be better than yesterday because..." I would focus on the "wins" I had from the day before. I would write about the friends and family that came to visit me. I would write about my schedule for the day.

You can write about whatever you choose. I recommend writing it from a positive mindset. If it is a time of chaos and confusion you can write out the "issue" at hand, then write about how you are either going to let it go, make it better, or how you are going to overcome and be triumphant. You get to choose.

"Writing in a journal reminds you of your goals and of your learning in life. It offers a place where you can hold a deliberate, thoughtful conversation with yourself." -- Robin S. Sharma

When life threw me a "curb" I took it on fully, had FAITH that everything would work out as God meant it to be, remained PRESENT in the mindful morning process that LAUNCHED me to go from Fractured to Remission.

Whatever you are going through at this time, I challenge you to begin by taking these three steps, followed by adding a daily morning routine that works for you. Just try it for 30 days and see what happens.

* * *

Gina Estrada is an Author, Speaker and Financial Consultant. Gina is a dedicated advisor who is truly committed to helping families, professionals and business owners help take control of their financial future. She is also an incredible cancer warrior and survivor, who works hard to empower women and those who will receive the worst news of their life. She is an inspiration and a walking beacon of hope to those around her. Be on the lookout for her upcoming book, "When Life Throws You a Curb: 10 tips for the Cancer Patient and Those Who Care."

ONLY THE BEGINNING
Susan Ackerman

I was 18 years old when Bob and I married. Babies having babies, we had no idea about love, relationships, parenting, or life. We both came from dysfunctional homes and couldn't wait to be on our own, living a life on our terms, where we could finally be grown-ups. My husband enlisted in the Army and we spent our first seven years together traveling the world, trying to figure out these things called marriage, parenting, and life.

I wouldn't say we were good at it, as a matter of fact, we did most things wrong. Neither of us had good role models growing up and so we struggled over the years with anger, dishonesty, and contempt. Neither of us understood how to deal with conflict so our arguments turned into assaults that were both verbal and physical. When it was over, we made up and life went on.

I was a stay-at-home mom to our three daughters and Bob worked hard outside the home to provide a good living for our family. We rarely did things together or as a family, it was just easier for us to stay apart.

My daughters grew and I was consumed with their activities. Girl Scout leader, chauffeur, and cheerleader to their endeavors, I attended their events and revolved my life completely around theirs. Having absolutely no relationship with my own mother, I was determined to give my daughters a better life. It was my purpose, and in my mind, it was always about them. I don't believe I ever really considered questioning whether or not I was happy.

During those years, I (Susan) did not exist. I was Mom and I was Wife... nothing more. My identity was wrapped in theirs. Years went by, my daughters grew, and my marriage to their father became more and more distant. Angry words, hurtful tones, and sheer disdain consumed our interactions with each other. I had never even considered whether our life was abnormal or unhealthy or that things could be different, or that I even deserved different. Remember, it was never about me.

Something changed, however, in October of 2002. We were married nearly 20 years at the time, roommates coexisting in the same home together, avoiding each other as much as we could. Our oldest daughter Tanya was 20 and in college, Nicole was 14 and Heather was 12.

It was a beautiful fall day and both headlights on my 1995 dark green Plymouth Voyager (my 'mom mobile') had burnt out. Because I was chauffeur to my younger daughters, I needed the lights fixed that afternoon before they cheered at the High School football game that night.

Bob was always good with cars and did most any repairs himself. The van bulbs would be no different, except they weren't cooperating and he was having a hard time. I was standing in the front doorway watching and Heather was close by, watching television in the living room.

After Bob struggled with the bulbs and uttered a few angry choice words, he looked over to me, with a cold and uncaring look on his face, and in a very calm voice said, "I hate you. I mean, I really fucking hate you. I fucking hate everything about you."

It was slow, it was deliberate, and it felt like a knife stabbing my heart.

My immediate knee-jerk reaction was to open the screen door and yell something just as hurtful, just as powerful back to him. I wanted to stand up for myself, have the last word, try to hurt him as he had hurt me, but just as my hand grabbed for the knob, Heather came up behind me and said, "Don't do it, Mom. Just ignore him. It's not worth it."

Such simple words, such a simple and profound request from my daughter. I looked at her and her face was pleading with me not to say anything. I stopped. I looked back out at him one last time and then I turned and walked away, never saying a word. But something changed within me at that very moment in time. I realized that my daughter, this 12-year-old young, suggestible girl, wanted me to ignore her father's behavior because it was *normal* to her. She didn't want me to fight it, she didn't want me to stand up for myself, she wanted to sweep it under the rug and simply forget it.

Please know, this is in no way meant to bash my ex-husband or even stick up for him. After a lot of soul-searching and forgiveness, today I realize that we were simply two imperfect people living in an imperfect marriage. It was a relationship turned cold.

This conversation was a wakeup call to how he truly felt and forced me to make a decision on how I wanted to live. Looking at my young, impressionable daughter, I knew that she deserved more. I knew that all of my daughters deserved more. I would eventually come to realize, though much later, that I deserved more.

This one moment in time, his cold, honest words, and my daughter's pleading voice created a light within me. Although just a flicker at first, it was a light that awakened a thought and eventually started a movement in my life.

I wondered how many women lived "normal" lives of sweeping things under the rug. I wondered how many women listened to those messages of hatred and disdain, who believed they were not good enough, smart enough or valuable enough. I wondered how many women believed that they were less than, that they were unlovable or unworthy. I wondered how many women were living lives of quiet desperation, scared to venture forward, scared of failure, deeply afraid that the voices might be right. I wondered how many women out there were just like me. And I wondered, how many daughters were watching them?

I cried that night and for weeks later for my daughters, for the messages they had received already. I cried for my marriage, that it had become such a desolate place for both of us, and I cried for all those women who I knew were silently crying in their own homes wondering the same thoughts, feeling the same fear that I was.

That one conversation, that one urging by my daughter, opened my eyes to a bigger picture. I knew that I had to break the cycle of hatred and dysfunction. I knew that it was up to me to give my daughters a message that women deserve better and that it is not okay to have a partner speak to them like that, even if I was not sure yet that I fully believed it myself. I realized that sweeping it under the rug and choosing to *ignore* the situation was not a normal or healthy way to live.

In that one moment, when my daughter told me to let it go, I pictured her being in a home with a partner who said those same words to her. I imagined the pain she would feel in her heart, the exact pain I was feeling. I could see her just simply walking away, choosing to ignore the behavior, going into her room and silently crying for her partner to love her, and accepting that perhaps she was not worthy of the love she desired. I could not bear to have my daughters live that same life. I had to set the example.

It was not for me, but for them that I devised a plan. I wasn't sure where to start. I did not have a degree to fall back on. I knew I would need to get a job, save money, find a place to live and move forward alone. I was petrified. I had never lived on my own before. What if all those people who told me I was useless and that I couldn't make it on my own were right? What if my husband was right when he told me I was nothing without him and that he owned me?

Crazy to realize that I never gave much thought to those voices as they were saying those things to me. I chose instead to ignore them, just as my daughter had asked me to do now. I told myself I didn't care what they said. I figured if I ignored them, it meant they couldn't get to me. I was wrong. What a realization to learn that these voices, whether I ignored them or not, withered away at my soul, tearing away any confidence or self-esteem that existed, and left me a puddled mess of doubt and insecurity. This new plan meant coming face-to-face with those voices, wondering if they were true, petrified of the unknown, but committed to a new life for my girls.

I prayed... a lot! I prayed for strength, I prayed for opportunities, I prayed for the right doors to open for me. I cried out in desperation from my bed each night, wondering if I was worthy enough or capable enough to see this through. And during the day, I submitted resumes and went on interviews. After only a few short months, in February, I obtained a job in a medical billing office and found myself working my first full-time job in a very long time.

Being out of the house and beginning my own life was difficult but fun for me. Of course, I was still living in the same house as my husband, so this was simply a baby step of venturing out. I started meeting new friends, I was making money – with the opportunity for a lot of overtime, and I was gaining confidence. My girls were doing well, my marriage had become even more silent, and I was able to put money in the bank. I started a layaway with new furniture, I started buying household items I would need when I moved, and I was working my plan. I still cried often. I was petrified of what this change would look like, but I prayed for strength and guidance along the way.

It took over a year and a half, but the time came and I was ready. A house became available four doors down from the girls' high school. It was perfect. I applied and was approved. Within two days I was planning my move and within a week, I had rented a U-Haul and moved myself and the girls into the home.

The first few weeks were busy, unpacking, decorating, and making the house my own. I was proud of myself for the progress I made. My daughters were adjusting to this new life and making the most of the changes. Once life settled, however, the loneliness set in. Funny thing, I was no stranger to loneliness. I had always felt such intense loneliness while living within my marriage, but this feeling was deeper. It was as if I was surrounded by a dark hole that was consuming me and the fears and doubts that I had so painfully ignored were poking and prodding my body. Voices screamed in my head, now what? I started wondering how I could make it on my own. What if I was alone forever? What if he was right? What if my parents were right? What had I done?

I realize now that God always has a plan, even if we don't always see it at first. In my aloneness, on a very desolate New Year's Eve, I reached out to a ministry for other divorced, widowed, and separated people. Little did I know that this ministry, made up of wounded healers, would change my life.

People just like myself, finding themselves in a new life, having to grieve the old and figure out exactly what the new life looked like. People who lost their identity and were forging a new reality. People in pain, hurting, fearful, and not sure how they would make it through.

People just like me. They were my tribe and through my participation, I began to find my voice, my worth, and my passion. I realized I was not alone and I learned that there was so much more to me than I had ever imagined. Like an onion, layers and layers of limited beliefs, fears, and sadness were peeled away.

I cried and grieved for the life I walked away from and the woman I thought I was. I began to see a new person, a woman who had dreams and aspirations of her own. I realized I had a voice and a purpose, and that my marriage, which once held me back and imprisoned in a world of fear and sadness, could actually be a stepping stone to propel me forward.

It was exciting, and like a flower in springtime, I could feel myself start to bloom into something new and different. I had confidence for the first time in my life. I was happy -- I mean, really happy. I started replacing those voices that held me down for so long with new messages of hope and inspiration. My life was joyful, I was at peace with myself, and life seemed new and exciting.

Within a year of being on my own, my oldest daughter one day over lunch asked me if I had found someone. The difference was becoming obvious to everyone around me. I simply laughed and answered her, "Yes, I found ME."

Fast forward 13 years later, to today. My daughters are strong, independent, incredible women. They each own their voice and live life on their own terms. I could not be prouder of the women they have become. All three have a heart for serving others and strive to make a difference.

Remember Heather, that young impressionable girl who told me to ignore her father that day so many years ago? Well, she is now a voice for the oppressed, a fighter for people's rights, and fearless in her pursuit of fairness. She speaks her truth and is not ever afraid to use her voice and stand up for what she believes in.

Sure, there are still some wounds there and insecurities that run deep and voices that rear their ugly heads from time to time, but these young women are inspirations to me as I watch them create a life that is so very different from mine. And for that, I am so thankful.

As for me, following the healing work of the ministry that changed my life, I moved across the state and eventually across the country, from a small-town girl in Pennsylvania with no dreams or desires to a Direct Sales Leader and eventually Women's Empowerment Coach in Reno, Nevada.

I work with women who are ready to dream big, play big, and live a life of purpose. I am blessed to help women find their voice, embrace their own uniqueness, and live the life they were created for. It is a life I could not have imagined when I stood in the doorway that afternoon listening to those hateful words of my husband and the urgings of a young girl who knew nothing different.

It's been an incredible ride and one that I wouldn't change for the world. Every setback, every pain, every tear has brought me to where I am today. Every part of my past colors my present, but I now realize that my past does not define my future.

And this message is one that needs to be shared, needs to be heard, and needs to be embraced. Women need to know that they are *not* their limited beliefs, and each belief that holds them back can and should be challenged. Women need to know that we are more than the voices in our head that tell us we aren't good enough, we aren't smart enough, we aren't pretty enough, thin enough, young enough, old enough, worthy enough or valuable enough. We need to scream from the rooftops, teach our daughters, and never forget that WE ARE ENOUGH just as we are...

A while back, while driving to an event, I noticed a field of dandelions. Back in the east, dandelions are everywhere, and most people consider a dandelion to be an annoying weed that just keeps coming back no matter how hard we try to kill them. I started thinking about these little flowers/weeds and decided to do a little research. I found that the dandelion is unique among flowers. It begins as a seedling, transforms into a yellow bud, and then again into a seedling. Folklore suggests that a dandelion is a way to symbolize life and the ups, and downs that come with it.

"In the midst of the grassy meadows, a dandelion stalk stands tall, displaying to the world its beautiful radiant glow." -- Author unknown.

This can represent our struggle to make a mark in this world, to stand high and tall in life, regardless of what may come. Then, when the storms of life blow against this delicate flower, its seedlings go with the wind, only to find a place where they can find nourishment and grow back again in abundance.

Isn't that how it is for us? Aren't women just like the dandelion? We stand tall as we enter the real world, trying to make our mark. We are strong, we are confident, we are fearless. But then life happens, the storms come, the setbacks halt us in our tracks, fear steps in and so often the voices of doubt scream in our ears, share lies of who we are, and we are scattered into broken pieces flying in many directions.

But the joy of the dandelion is that it takes root where it lands, it finds nourishment where it is and blooms again, stronger, taller and bolder than before. And that, my friend, is me and you and so many other women we know. We, like the dandelions, can bloom again when the storms of life happen. We can use our setbacks as an end or a new beginning.

Looking back to that younger Susan, standing in the doorway of her home on that beautiful October afternoon, being blown down by the storm that is life, I thought it was the end. Now I realize that it was only the beginning.

* * *

Susan Ackerman is a phenomenal woman, with an incredibly powerful story to tell. She is an author, speaker, motivator and survivor. Empowering women to find their voice and their purpose is what she was meant to do. Susan studied at Chatham University and Life and Transition Coaching at IPEC. She is currently the Director of "Inspire Reno" - an Entrepreneurial Development Center for women. Her mission is to provide a positive and creative environment where women can grow both personally and professionally. In addition to building Inspire Reno, Susan's new program "Encouragement by the Cup" will be starting soon, offering women the opportunity to join her once a week – virtually – for a weekly dose of "encouragement." She is working on publishing her first self-help book, the first of many to come.

LEARNING TO LAUNCH MYSELF

Joe Koronowski

The door buzzed as my friend Barron swiped his ID badge at the entrance of the NASA Mission Control Center (MCC). "Close your mouth... breathe, don't be a dork." He kept saying to me as we toured the MCC training, testing, and flight control facilities as well as the historic Apollo Space Flight control room where the team in the MCC landed men on the moon.

I did not know the challenges that lay ahead; the training, the studying, the knowledge and skills needed to pass the three levels of certification to be a Flight Controller for the Manned Space Flight program for which I was now a part of. It would take thousands of hours of studying and training and countless sleepless nights. But there I stood, I was at NASA! I did not know until much later that I was going to create history every time I went to work with the men and women I met that day behind those Mission Control doors.

Me! A farm boy from a little town in upstate New York! It was overwhelming to think how far I'd come and how uncomfortably out of place I felt as Barron showed me around various rooms, attempted to explain each control console's duty, the software and the space flight hardware. I was seeing all this for the first time, knowing that I was soon going to be asked to know all about how to operate each piece.

Just a few years before that tour, my future as an engineer looked like it may never happen. It was the end of my first semester at Texas A&M. I had just left the Dean of Mechanical Engineering's Office in Zachary Hall. His words were still ringing in my ears, "Joe, I know this is your first semester here at A&M, I want you to be successful but your grades are not very good. You will be placed on academic probation starting next semester. If your grades do not improve we will have to ask you to leave. You have some choices to make young man…"

I was in shock, bewildered, and numb. Did I have a future as an Aggie? As an engineer? Slowly I walked down the angled concrete steps in front of Zachary Hall. I don't remember if I looked both ways or if I used a crosswalk, but I managed to get across Spence Street without getting hit by a car. I stopped in the quad area between the Engineering/Physics and the Geology buildings and looked down at the grade sheet the Dean had given me. GPA: 0.5 pts. I was failing. I was crushed, and if not for the sheet of paper in my hands I wouldn't have believed it, I had worked my tail off in all my classes. Was I going to fail out of Texas A&M?

For what may have been only 5-10 minutes but seemed like an eternity, I stood in the quad looking at my grade report. This time I felt different than any other challenge prior to this one. I realized I was on my own, for maybe the first time in my life. Reaching out to my sister for comfort, asking my brother for advice or leaning heavily on my mom, dad or grandfather was no longer an option. There in the quad with a blur of students passing by, not noticing me or my blank stare, I had my very first "Come to Jesus Conversation" with myself.

Deep down inside I knew that my old ways were no longer an option. The decision I was about to make for my life was a pivotal point, a defining moment that would alter the trajectory of my future forever. The dean was right, I did have some choices to make. If I couldn't get my grades up he recommended two choices, either find another university or find a major other than Engineering. That was like telling a farmer not to get dirty. That is who we are and what we do!

I loved mechanical things. In my mind I could see in 3-D and color. I would take things apart just to see how they worked, then put them back together and make them work better. Machines fascinated me. The exactness of calculations excited me. As a child, a ruler, sharp pencil and a piece of paper offered hours of intrigue. I would draft things with exact precision. That pastime led me to get my Associates Degree in drafting and inspired the desire to learn more. I wanted to study engineering!

The Dean didn't count on a few things, my desire and my passion for all things mechanical and what it means to be a farmer. Farmers roll their sleeves up, set their mind on a task without worrying how big or how long it will take. They gather the needed items then set upon the task to do whatever it takes for as long as it takes. Whether it is to cultivate the land, grow crops, care for animals or repair machines or buildings, farmers seek to ultimately achieve the goal no matter the weather or how hard it is. As my father would say, "The hay is not going to bail itself."

I am a product of my upbringing and my environment, as well as my natural talents. In a family of six kids, I was always getting into some mischief. Some events occurred that could have turned tragic while living life in New York. Such as falling from a large tree with nothing more than a few scratches, slipping through the ice of a river in winter, or just falling off my bike as it flew uncontrollably down a steep embankment.

I also failed out of second grade and felt the pressure of being the middle boy in a family of six. As my sister said, since she is the only girl, I am the middle kid. During one extreme mischief moment as a 9-year-old boy, I accidentally burned myself over 20% of my body with kerosene by pouring the fluid onto a hot bed of coals from a campfire.

These challenges I encountered as a young boy shaped me in ways I could not see. I see them now as what God presented to me to teach me a choice, to challenge me, to test my resolve. I could have given up, cried. I could have run away to be safe as I did many times. I could have blamed others as I also did. I could have been mad at God or even given in and committed suicide from a very dark place and time in my life. For some reason I chose differently. Early in my teens I wondered why I did not die when I was on fire. I feel I was unconsciously curious and feared I would miss out on some really cool stuff life has to offer.

My mother was the unconditional love in my life, supporting me to be exactly who I wanted to be. My father was adamantly militant about safety yet focused on getting the job done. He taught me to operate a chainsaw at a young age and work with heavy equipment through experiential learning. "Joe, climb up on this backhoe and let me show you how to dig this hole. This lever moves the bucket, this moves the arm and this is how you take a scoop of rock and dump the rock over here. Okay, now you dig the rock."

That was how dad was, he taught my brothers and me how to do, so there were many hands working in a skilled way toward a common goal. This is why I am as skilled as I am. My father provided the opportunity for me to see, feel, learn and experience life that fulfilled my passion of curiosity to know how and why, as well as my intellectual desire to learn. As a young man, by the time I was 16 years old I led a very experientially rich life. I was exposed to hundreds of different hands-on trades by living on the farm with my father.

From that place of curiosity, adaptability and always getting the work done as a farmer, I decided there was a third choice at Texas A&M, one of which the Dean probably didn't think me capable. I chose to use my passion, my desire and my farmer work ethic to do whatever it took to complete the work. To graduate with an engineering degree.

The skill I already possessed was my work ethic. This skill had successfully taken me through community college in Utica, New York and landed me at Texas A&M. I had relied heavily on my old-fashioned farm-boy work ethic of hard work and long hours to get any job done. That first semester I figured that if I put in enough hard work and time it would pay off. What I didn't realize was that I had to put in the time on the right things to create success in my life.

It didn't take long to see that work ethic and long hours were not going to be enough anymore. The direction I took was to figure out what those other things were to be successful. I was going to graduate with a Mechanical Engineering degree, so I set off to the campus student services office to seek advice and help to learn how this thing called 'college' worked.

Student services was a great place to start. I didn't know what I didn't know. My ability to work hard and long was important, but I had to put that effort into the tasks that would get me the results that were needed -- not only to graduate, but first just to pass a semester so I could stay in college. I had to learn how to take notes in class efficiently and even more important, how to study those notes. I suffered greatly from test anxiety and had to learn how to prepare enough and in a way that gave me confidence on test day.

I learned how I learn best for me. For example, I had to sit in the front and center of class, so I wouldn't get distracted by other students. I raised my hand and asked a lot of questions. It may have annoyed the rest of the class because my hand always shot up, but I wanted to understand everything.

I also learned that Practice makes you better. This is where I began to learn the beginnings of Mastery: "Repetitive and purposeful actions over time creates Mastery." Even as a kid I was always afraid I would miss out on something. Dad would be ready to go out the door and I yearned to go with him. From a very young age, I possessed an almost insatiable curiosity. Every chance I got I accompanied my dad to witness what he was doing and to learn as much as I could about farming and life.

In college and on into working towards certification as a Flight Controller at NASA, it wasn't an option to say "I don't know;" I had to know and I had to figure out a way to learn it. I discovered how to do research at A&M and I couldn't get enough. It turns out, almost failing out of college might have been the best thing to happen to me.

As an introvert who kept to myself, discovering study groups was life-changing. I met people like me who were struggling and were willing to help others learn and pass the tests. WOW! With these newfound skills, my student life exploded. I was learning what I needed to do to not only survive, but thrive in college, and it turns out, life.

Things started to turn around. I quickly began to excel and I gained a reputation for saying "yes." During that next semester in my materials lab the Teaching Assistant told us of the school's plan to build and enter a solar powered car in the Sunrayce Challenge. This was a solar car race for university students to build and race a car across various parts of the United States. I looked at our professor and said, "Yes!"

That decision led me to meet the people that would eventually open the path to Mission Control. As I began to make decisions that would alter the course of my life, my "internal leader" showed up. Part of being a good leader is knowing in your heart what the right move is, for you. That day in the quad I chose for me. I had spent my life following what other people expected of me, doing what other people told me to do. That day I began to rely on myself and to look inside to discover what I truly wanted.

Those lessons I learned at Texas A&M enabled me to stay in school and to graduate with an Engineering degree. But they also led me to NASA's Mission Control. That tour with Barron was just the beginning of my journey at NASA.

In order to become a Mission Lead, or even gain the security clearance to enter the flight control room of MCC un-escorted by a certified Flight Controller, I had to pass three different certifications. There were thousands of acronyms and technical aspects to memorize. I had to know how the systems from other console positions interfaced with mine. I had to know how the hardware operated right down to the software codes. I had to learn what each and every command sent to the ISS from my console was supposed to do, and when it did not provide the expected outcome, how to troubleshoot the hardware to fix it. It was like I was in college all over again, but this time I knew how to succeed.

There were thousands of hours of self-study and group study, hundreds of hours of practice through Training Simulations. This just scratched the surface of what my training entailed. We were evaluated on such nebulous standards as, Console Presence. This was whether or not you could lead under pressure, and whether you had the steely-eyed missile man presence required to be an ECLSS (Environmental Controls and Life Support Systems) Officer for NASA.

Manned Space Flight Operations Directorate. The position I wanted was to be an officer for the Environmental Controls and Life Support Systems. I would be in charge of monitoring and ensuring the atmosphere was safe and habitable for the astronauts. The team was also in charge of -- and the authors of -- the 'Complex Space Craft Emergency Operations Handbook,' better know as "The Red Book." The procedures in that book and the training the team provided helped the astronauts to follow the protocol during an emergency aboard the ISS that could save their lives.

The many months and thousands of hours seemed to rush by. I was drinking from a fire hose of knowledge as fast as I could to not only learn all knowledge, but to be able to access it in a 'nanosecond of a thought' when I got on console in MCC. There was no learning curve, it was 90 degrees straight up. There were many that weren't able, or meant to climb what I started calling "the brick wall." But I kept climbing.

I had passed two of the three levels of my certification to be a Mission Control, Flight Controller. The third level was like graduating with your doctorate degree. The day I finished my final simulation I went in to talk to my boss,

Kwatsi. He tried to put on a good poker face with me after asking me how I thought the final ECLSS simulation went. Listening to my reply, he couldn't control how happy he was.

During a final certification simulation, a Flight Director chaperone sits on console with you. They sit with you during the entire simulation to observe console operations and actions first hand. My Flight Director chaperone, Sally, had stopped by Kwatsi's office on her way out to tell him how well I did. She was completely confident in my console presence and my knowledge. He relayed this to me in his steely-eyed missile man way, eventually letting me know... I had passed! That was one of the most amazing days in my life.

Leaving his office that day, I might not have remembered the dean of engineering's office I left years before, but now, looking back, it's interesting to see the difference of those two pivotal life moments. When I left the dean's office I could have run away, hid, cried, blamed others, been mad at God and given up. That's always a choice during life's challenges. But I chose a different path.

Almost failing out of college challenged me to grow in ways I never expected, but I didn't give up. I was confident in who I really was and I relied on me. I worked hard, I learned how to put the effort into the right things and made my curiosity work for me. I learned to be my internal leader and launched myself: from stalling and failing, to Mission

Control. That first time I "badged" into NASA's Mission Control Center, unescorted, as a Certified ECLSS (Environmental Control and Life Support Systems) officer was a surreal and proud moment.

Over the years, badging into Mission Control in Houston became a normal part of my day. After badging in, the day's activities were never routine as a Flight Controller for the International Space Station. I never knew what interesting challenge I might encounter when I entered those doors, but I knew this farm-boy from upstate New York had evolved into a strong, internal leader who could handle whatever he encountered.

"Achieving a goal is not as much about the goal; as it is always about whom you must become to achieve the goal."

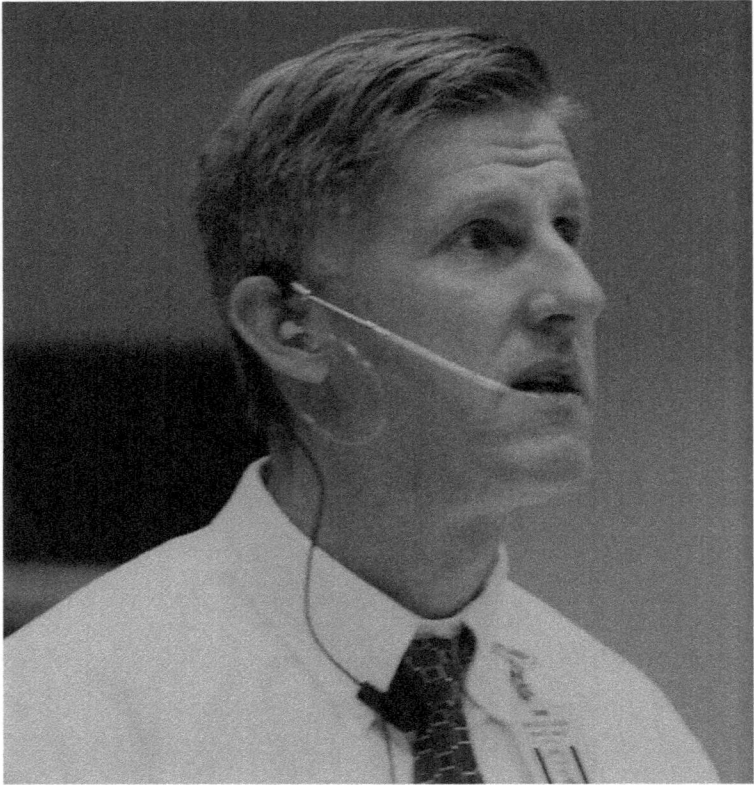

* * *

Joe is a "Recovering Rocket Scientist" whose journey through life continues to inspire others while he continues on his mission. Joe shares his life experiences from growing up on a farm in New York to reaching the heights of NASA Mission Control. Joe went back to school to pursue his second degree, Engineering, at Texas A&M. He is now an Author, Speaker, and Motivator. Joe will paint a picture of his incredible rise to success and his journey along the way. His greatest purpose is to inspire you to never give up on yourself. Joe demonstrates how simple it is to transform your dreams into your reality! www.321launchyourlife.com

WARRIOR RISING

Fran Tone

"I have been fighting since I was a child.
I am not a survivor. I am a warrior
The devil whispered ... you cannot withstand the storm.
The warrior replied: I am the storm.
I am a warrior
I will get through the storm
I will show the storm who is boss
I will show everyone
I am stronger than all things that have hurt me
Stronger than my past
Stronger than the challenges that are coming in the future
I don't invite those challenges, but I also don't back down
from them
I know we all face tough times
I know I'm not exempt from life's struggles
But I also know I am strong
I know this will pass
I know there will be better days
But only if I keep fighting."
FearlessMotivation.com
***I just wish the sword and shield weren't so heavy;
I'm getting tired holding them up all the time***

On Thanksgiving night 2005, dinner was done and
the TV was off. Everyone had gone to bed. The house was
quiet except for the kitchen sink as I washed every dish, fork,
spoon, knife, glass, cup, pot and pan. My mind wasn't quiet
though. It was racing with the thought of pulling out an
international number and dialing.

My stomach was in knots as I kept washing and drying. I put away every dish, fork, spoon, knife, glass, cup, pot and pan. I turned off all the lights downstairs and was about to head upstairs to bed. I looked in my office. I looked at the phone on my desk. I sat down and looked again at the phone on my desk. I pulled out a folded piece of paper and opened it. I stared at the number on the paper. I got up to check on the clean kitchen several times.

I was suffering from what I call, "my father is going to leave me again" feeling. It's that feeling I get when I think I'm going to be hurt badly again, physically, emotionally or mentally. It was a familiar feeling. I don't have a specific memory of that feeling when my Japanese mother died and my American father left when I was only a year old. I can't recall that feeling when my Japanese grandmother put me up for adoption at age five to a childless couple made up of a Japanese woman and an American man. But I do recall having that feeling shortly after my first American friends taunted me, yelling, "your mother is dead, your mother is dead" repeatedly, the way some children can be unknowingly cruel.

I didn't have the feeling at the point of taunting. The feeling came across that evening when my parents sat me down for a talk and I discovered that it was true: my mother was dead and these parents whom I thought had finally come back to get me were imposters. I wasn't even six. My adoptive father told me how special I was because I had been chosen. And soon thereafter, I found out how special I really was when my adoptive father entered my bedroom one night. Lights were out. I should have been asleep, but I wasn't. He began to touch me in ways I didn't understand. I was afraid to protest. Later, my adoptive father told me this was our secret.

Faced with no one to protect me, and harboring a secret, I was alone. Yet, despite what happened at night, I would get up each morning and tackle the day. During summer months, I'd go out to play and I played hard. I became accomplished on monkey bars, cross bars and any obstacle I could find. I even climbed massive boulders in slippers. I would get injured, but the pain didn't bother me. I felt I owned the local medical staff and they could fix anything that physically hurt me.

During winter months, I went to school and became an over-achiever. I tackled life obsessively to get the prize. If there was a pin, certificate, medal or trophy, I went for it and usually got it. And on the few occasions when I didn't get a prize, it left an open wound to remind me to fight harder. It seems I was always at war with the world and I protected little ol' me carefully. I didn't let anyone in. My public person became what I thought others expected. I quickly grew a shell around myself, never to let anyone see the real me because often I felt so small. If someone saw the real me, I might disappear.

In elementary, middle and high school, I was always the "new kid." My adoptive father was in the Army and we moved every three years. I started high school in one state and finished in another state. My last 2 ½ years of high school was spent with a group of students who had known each other since kindergarten. I didn't fit in and the girls let me know with certainty that I would never fit in. I was still alone. By then, it didn't matter much to me, or so I thought. After all, I was still getting the prizes and I was getting accustomed to being alone.

I was 20 years old. My father grew tired of my constant telephone calls with my then boyfriend and decided I should be married. He drove me halfway across the country and left me with my boyfriend to be married.

That trip was the last time he touched me. I gave up a full college scholarship, gave up school and got married. As you can imagine, that marriage did not last. Unfortunately, being married didn't change me. I was still alone, and my shell grew thicker. At first, I thought my husband was going to be my protector. But his mother disliked me and made no apology for mistreating me. My husband's reaction was I should just put up with it, so I did. Staying silent, I once again found myself alone.

I then went off to Germany to be a respectable officer's wife (my husband was an Army Officer). Once there, I participated in the Officers' Wives Club. I volunteered, met people, smiled, laughed, shook hands. I imagined that if I performed well as an officer's wife, maybe I wouldn't be alone. I discovered that wasn't going to be the case.

A few months after arriving in Germany, I suffered a near-fatal car accident. In addition to many injuries, my ribs had broken and cut one kidney into several pieces. When I began uncontrollably bleeding internally, I was taken into emergency surgery, where doctors spent 14 hours putting me back together. My entire abdomen was opened and put back together with stitches and staples. After the surgery, I stayed bedridden for three weeks and had to learn to walk all over again. I couldn't even get out of bed without assistance. My injury put my husband and me to the top of the housing list so that we could be given base housing and be closer to the military medical center.

When the day approached to move our household from an off-base apartment 20 minutes away, my husband's commander decided to send my husband home from a field exercise for one day to help me. All the men in his unit had been gone almost a month on a field exercise and they were not coming home for a few more weeks. By then, I could roll onto my stomach, slide myself out of bed, and from all fours, pull myself up by holding onto the mattress to get up. When

I walked, I was still hunched over because it was too painful to stand upright.

The day before my husband was to return home to help me move, I was approached by the commander's wife and several other young officers' wives all around my age, complaining that it was unfair for me to see my husband when they had to go without. I recall marveling at the lack of compassion and selfishness heading my way while I stood by the mail room grimacing in pain. I felt alone again. My shell grew thicker.

Shortly after, I wrote a long letter to my mother-in-law apologizing for the lack of communication and explaining all that had happened. While my husband was still in the field, I received a 10-page scathing letter from my mother-in-law. I could hear her screaming at me from the pages about what a horrible woman I was because I must be preventing my husband from communicating with her. I remember crying hard, despite the pain in my abdomen, because it hurt so much to be accused so wrongly. I was facing so much pain and once again doing it alone.

My solace was found in prizes. My prizes consisted of admiration and praise. After I was able to stand upright and felt well again, I bounced back, playing tennis daily for eight hours, even though I was pregnant, much to the marvel of those around me. I recovered from the accident and delivered a healthy 7 lb. 6 oz. little boy. During pregnancy, I had gained 55 pounds (despite all that tennis). When I left the hospital, I had not lost a single pound. That seemed physically impossible in my mind, but I had to face the weight gain. I took up racquetball and lost 55 pounds in 3 months. Imagine how envious other women were to my fast weight loss and the praises they spoke! Meanwhile, I was a dutiful Army officer's wife who cooked lavishly and entertained with a keen eye for display.

My prizes were the compliments I received from all guests who came. By my mid-20's, I had become an accomplished host, athlete, officer's wife and mother. I found prizes whenever and wherever I could find them. Dangle a "medal" in front of me and I'd do whatever it took.

Later, now stateside, I needed a job. Despite having no experience or education, I applied for a position as a legal secretary. With nothing to back me up, I told the lawyers that I'd be the best legal secretary they had ever seen. I knew that I could over-achieve because that is what I did. My prize was the lawyers claiming I was the best they had ever known. Soon, I became a self-made paralegal and my prize was to become a top paralegal and office administrator.

I finally divorced and married my current husband, a lawyer, who has been a rock for me. However, I didn't tell him about my past. I still kept all my secrets. Somehow, he had seen glimmers of little ol' me through the thick, hard shell of protection I had spent a lifetime building and latched onto those glimmers. He also knew that I always dreamt of being a lawyer.

I can remember when the idea came to me to become a lawyer. I was only 14 years old. I had been watching episodes of Perry Mason, a television drama about a criminal defense attorney who was kind, smart and trusted by everyone. That's what I wanted. In my youthful mind, I figured out that if I couldn't protect myself, I could help others instead. Even though I trusted no one, I wanted others to trust me. Oddly enough, it worked. My husband finally encouraged me to go to law school, so I went. I graduated at the top of my class and have the plaques to show off as prizes.

After I became a lawyer, I worked hard to gain the trust of judges, other lawyers and my clients. I even had some difficulty with professional responsibility exams because I would expect more of myself than was required and I'd get the answer wrong! You can imagine that this prize-seeker wasn't too happy about that. At first, it seemed odd that I would choose a profession that is publicly shunned for lack of trust but internally is one in which trust is a foundational rock. And I learned quickly how to develop trust even while I still hid deep within my shell. As a lawyer, I could pull out my sword and shield and go to battle for others.

I also became a ski instructor in my 40's. And that gave me another resource to go after prizes. I got my bronze Level 1 certification pin, then my silver Level 2 certification pin. As I was nearing 50, I pushed hard to get the coveted "gold pin," the highest level certified ski instructor, competing against 20- and 30-year-olds.

In my mid-50's I trained hard to become a podium-finishing standup paddleboard racer and was coming in first in my division consistently. I have lots of trophies to show for that accomplishment. It didn't seem to matter how my life went, as long as I was collecting prizes, I felt I was succeeding in life. But I still felt alone. Then on that Thanksgiving night in 2005, my life turned around. I can't say everything changed overnight, but I can pinpoint that time as the moment when I and my life began to change.

That international number was the telephone number for my biological father, Bill, who had left me when I was one year old, shortly after my biological mother passed away. I was raised by my Japanese grandmother until I was five, when I was adopted. By 2005, my adoptive parents had passed away. In fact, my adoptive father had just died in 2004. I knew a few things about Bill. I knew he had written a couple of books and had bit parts in movies filmed in Japan. I had read his books and watched the movies. I wondered if he was curious about what had happened to me. I worried a lot about the reaction I would get when he answered the phone. I worried he wouldn't answer the phone. I worried that his wife would answer the phone. I worried a lot. But I made the call.

Before making the call, I wrote down anything I thought I might say in Japanese and in English. Although Japanese was my first language, my adoptive mother stopped speaking Japanese to me when I was adopted for fear I'd have a strong accent. That was back in 1961, and what we know about language today wasn't common knowledge then. So my Japanese was pretty sketchy and that of a 5-year-old, at that.

It took me over an hour to write everything I wanted to say. I rehearsed the various sentences in Japanese so I could say them comfortably and correctly, with the correct accent to be understood. I had no idea who might answer the phone -- if it were answered at all. I didn't know if there'd be an answering machine so I wanted to leave a clear message in Japanese that could be understood. Recall that I got up several times to check on my clean kitchen. I suppose I was pretty nervous.

I also had to check the time. Thankful for the internet in 2005, I could easily determine that midnight in California was 4 PM in Japan. That seemed like a reasonable time to call Japan. So I picked up the phone and dialed. A female voice answered, "Moshi, moshi," (the common way Japanese answer the telephone). Yikes! I began to read the Japanese

136

words I had written down. I had no idea to whom I was speaking, but speculated that it was my father's wife. I told her my name and asked if my father (stating his name) was available.

The woman responded in Japanese, and from what little I could translate, the answer was "no, he's not here." I had anticipated this possibility. I had anticipated every possibility in detail -- in writing -- so I went to another sheet of paper and asked if I could leave a message for him to return my call. She responded, "Hai," (yes). I thanked her and gave her my "Denwa bango" (telephone number). She responded, "Hai," and abruptly ended the call. I hung up, gulped and stared at the phone, thinking this might be the end of nothing.

Less than fifteen seconds later, I was startled when the phone rang. I meekly answered, "Hello." (When I say "meekly," I mean *meekly*.)

A man's voice stated, "Hello, this is Bill ..."

I replied, "This is Francine and I am ..."

He quickly, and nicely interrupted, saying, "I know who you are, Francine."

Holy smokes! He knew who I was. Now what? My preparation had not gone that far. We talked. He was 80 years old now. He still lived in Tokyo. But he asked more questions and learned about me, what I was doing, where I lived, about my son who had graduated from the Air Force

137

Academy. My biological father was a retired Army military intelligence officer from World War II. I told him I was a lawyer, that I was happily married. I told him I lived in California and I skied.

We talked for over an hour. He sounded sincerely interested in what had happened to me. He sounded happy to talk to me. He never rushed the conversation. I felt he cared. I cried. In that instant, I forgave him for leaving me. I no longer cared about that.

I asked him, "Would it be okay if I came to Japan to meet you?"

He replied, "why wouldn't it be?"
That began my preparation and journey to Japan to meet him. I went to Japan. I met Bill. We met four times, with his wife and my husband along for the ride. I liked Bill. He had a sharp mind, even at 80. He shared his wisdom with me. We had a connection. I had no idea where this might go.

During our last meeting, he gave me an extended warm hug. I didn't realize at that moment that I would never see him again. During that same trip, I reconnected with my biological mother's family. I recognized my aunts and my uncle immediately and I met a bunch of cousins I didn't even know I had. When I caught up to my aunts, they were cleaning the gravesite where my grandmother's ashes were buried. Between tears and bowing, my aunts told my grandmother that she had been right that I would return. More tears.

That trip, when I reconnected with my real family, became a turning point in my life. I didn't feel alone anymore. My shell began to crack. Being alone … in your own silence … is a terrible place to be.

We hear of teenagers committing suicide because they felt alone in this world. Loneliness is one of the leading causes of suicidal ideations. And yes, during my teenage years, I thought about suicide almost every night. I was alone as an adult, which left me in long bouts of depression. I thought I was clinically depressed, but I didn't have time to deal with that because I had to put my energy toward getting prizes. Prizes were a poor substitute for a feeling of self-worth.

Loneliness comes not only from the feeling of being alone and left behind, but also from not being able to trust anyone in your life. I was always on guard. I could barely trust myself, much less anyone else. The outer shell grew and became thick. Oddly, my exterior mimicked the shell. My hair was perfectly styled. I wore clothes that were my business armor and sent the message not to mess with me. The outer image said "tough gal," all the while inside I remained small and alone.

Looking back, I've come to realize that I was a warrior all along. I didn't let what happened to me or around me limit what I needed to do. It didn't matter that the prize kept me going. I kept going. I kept fighting, even if I had no trust in anyone or anything. Despite feeling lonely much of my life, I got up every day and fought. Perhaps it was a good thing that I had prizes to fight for. Being a warrior got me through my life long enough to find a way out of loneliness. Until then, despite my accomplishments, I was insecure and self-conscious.

Today, I encapsulate my story by saying that I was orphaned at one, adopted at five, molested before I was six and lived that life until I got married. I felt alone, always. I should have been an alcoholic, drug addict or a prostitute, or dead at an early age, or all the above. But I wasn't. Why not?

My secret was the fact that I was a warrior. I didn't have a word for it when I was growing up, but the warrior within grew and I embraced her. That warrior had been growing and rising my entire life. But a warrior, alone, is not enough to live a fulfilled life. When I realized that loneliness had fueled the warrior and built a shell around me, I realized why the sword and shield were so heavy. One can act like a warrior for a lifetime but never feel like a warrior inside.

My inner warrior wanted to put the sword and shield down. They were so heavy, held together with prizes, medals and trophies. I needed to shed the weight. And when I found myself not alone, I could easily put down the sword and shield.

So who is this warrior? When I think of a warrior, the picture that comes to mind is a woman (because I happen to be a woman) wearing armor with a sword and shield. I sometimes see this warrior charging fiercely against her enemy. Sometimes I see her setting aside the sword and shield and tenderly cuddling a young child. Sometimes I see her in the corner weeping. These are all attributes of a warrior.

Some of my favorite movies, fantasies and shows are about warriors. I didn't realize how consistent my attraction to warriors was until I began asking myself the question: what helped me get through it all? Growing up, I used to watch samurai shows and root for the Japanese warrior. And yes, Mulan is one of my favorite Disney characters. Movies such as Gladiator, and television shows like Xena Princess Warrior were always on my must-watch list.

I embraced all of these warriors entirely, through glory and pain. I now embrace the strength and the vulnerability. I embrace the battle cries as well as the silent tears of loneliness and loss. I embrace the tender moments when I connect with someone else through their story or mine.

I believe we all have a warrior within and the warrior is not necessarily someone who charges with sword and shield. There must be a vulnerability. There must be lessons learned. Not everyone has tapped into the warrior. Some don't even know the warrior is there. Some never find it. Some find it only in desperate times. Some need help finding it.

By embracing the inner warrior in her entirety, my warrior grew and helped me through both good times and bad. My warrior gave me the tenacity to be successful in law school and as a lawyer. My warrior gave me the strength to standup paddle for 22 miles. My warrior gives me the discipline to stay a course. My warrior helped me conquer challenges.

Today, my warrior gives me the strength to reveal my weakness. My warrior gives me the insight to help others find their warrior. My life of triggering my warrior, day after day, year after year, gave me a tool that I could use. There were plenty of days when I forgot to tap into my warrior. But there were lots of days when I used my warrior to get through the day, week, month and year. The more I tapped into my warrior, the stronger she became.

My warrior gave me a sword and shield to protect myself until I came upon the day when I learned that I wasn't alone, that I could develop the capacity to trust and put down the sword and shield. My warrior saved me from a life path that could have destroyed me. Today, that same warrior is present, but not always battle ready. I feel free to share who I am, without obsessing over prizes. Life is lighter and more fulfilling without that heavy shell that I used to drag around.

I have been fighting since I was a child. I am not just a survivor, but I am a warrior. I am the storm in my own life. I can and do get through storms. I am stronger than all the things that have hurt me. I am stronger than my past. I am stronger than the challenges that I have not yet faced. I don't back down from life challenges. I know I will struggle at times. But I know I am strong. I know bad days will pass. I know better days are always ahead of me. I choose to keep fighting.

Today, I know I am even stronger because I have unleashed the entire warrior, not just the warrior who wields a sword and shield.

***

Francine Tone (FrancineTone.com is a speaker, author, advisor, attorney and athlete. She is a California lawyer and managing partner of her law firm, Tone & Tone (www.ToneandTone.com). Formerly a trial lawyer, today, as a certified appellate law specialist, she handles cases in courts of appeal and supreme courts and serves as a legal strategist for trial lawyers. She travels statewide offering ethics courses to lawyers. Her passion is to help non-lawyers have a positive experience navigating the legal system and she is the author of the #1 bestseller "What Every Good Lawyer Wants You to Know." She is a legal ethics, trust-building, leadership and productivity expert, bringing together the skills and habits of a successful business person and a peak performance athlete. She is also the author of the "How to Life Better Blog" (www.HowtoLifeBetter.com). She is an accomplished skier, ski instructor and trainer, a stand-up paddleboard racer and scuba divemaster. One of her favorite quotes is from Dr. Seuss: "You'll never be bored when you try something new. There's really no limit to what you can do!" Her latest challenges include singing, playing the ukulele and surfing her stand-up paddleboard. Francine has one son and lives with her husband/law partner in Truckee, California.

RAGE AGAINST THE DYING OF THE LIGHT

Clayton Lucas

April 24, 2009, was the day that is forever seared into the recesses of my memory as my worst day, before or since. My wife, Lora, would say the same for her.

As a police sergeant, I had just arrived at the station to supervise the graveyard patrol shift. I was preparing for that evening's briefing when my mobile phone rang. It was my wife, Lora. I typically would have called her back after the shift briefing was over but since we had not yet begun, I answered. In the most frantic, frightened voice I'd ever heard her speak.

"Willie's pediatrician just called and said that Willie has glucose in his urine and that it can potentially be life-threatening. Willie needs to go to the emergency room at Children's Hospital in Madera and the doctor said that minutes matter."

"Do you need me to get an ambulance?"

"The doctor said there's nothing an ambulance can do, Willie just needs to get there now."

"I'm on my way."

Willie was the youngest of our three boys. At the time, Clayton III was eight, Jonah who was six and Willie was 10 months old. He was the happiest baby we had ever seen, at least up until the week prior. He had been sick for days, causing him to be cranky and miserable. His symptoms were strange. He was drinking several large glasses of water per hour and soaking through an exorbitant number of diapers every day. The only thing that seemed to perk him up was ice cream. So, in an effort to ease his pain, I fed him ice cream several times per day, with not so much as an inkling that I was doing him more harm than good.

In all my years as a police officer, I had dealt with assailants that had fought me, assaulted me, attempted to stab me and had even shot at me and never had I been more scared. Lora's words, "minutes matter" resounded over and over in my mind like a broken record. By the time I hung up the phone, my heart felt as if it was going to beat out of my chest, my palms were sweating and I felt as though I were going to vomit, as my mind raced through what could possibly be wrong with my little boy. I literally ran to the police chief's office, grateful that he had not left for the day.

"Rich, Willie is sick. I have no idea what's wrong with him but the doctor said that minutes matter and there's nothing an ambulance can do for him!"

Rich told me to take my patrol car and get Willie to the hospital by any means necessary. I rushed home where Lora was holding Willie in our driveway waiting for me. She sat in the back seat with Willie on her lap. He was conscious but limp as he laid his head on her chest. I looked in the rearview mirror once to see Lora resting her face on the top of Willie's head, tears streaming down her cheeks. Not a word was said the entire trip as I focused on the road and getting to the hospital quickly and safely. With all the first responder training I had received throughout my career, I was not prepared for this.

We arrived at the emergency room of Children's Hospital in Madera, California in just over 20 minutes, a drive that normally took an hour. I quickly parked, threw the rear door open and snatched Willie out of Lora's arms, before sprinting through the entrance with Lora following closely behind. As we ran in, there was standing room only with a long line to the reception desk. We stood in line, anxious for someone to attend to us but I was disheartened knowing that we would have to wait our turn.

Like a song stuck in my head, the words, "minutes matter" continued playing over and over in my mind. I finally decided that Willie could not wait any longer. I stepped out of line and marched up to the reception counter, Willie's head on my chest, his arms and legs hanging like a ragdoll, and told the receptionist that his pediatrician had sent us and told us that "minutes matter." The receptionist asked me to get back in line and wait our turn. However, a nurse reviewing a chart behind the receptionist shouted, "That's our priority four. Get him back there now."

As scared as I had been up to that point, the urgency that I observed in the face of that nurse immediately took my breath away. In that moment, it all became very real. We followed the nurse through the double doors, to a private room where she asked me to place Willie on the bed. It was difficult for me to step back and not interfere, but I knew the nurse had a job to do and my involvement would only get in the way.

The nurse began checking Willie's vitals. I wanted so badly to ask what was wrong with him, but I didn't want to interrupt. Even more than that, I wanted to ask if my little boy was going to be okay, but I didn't dare. I was afraid of the answer. They immediately put an IV in his arm, yet Willie was so weak that he didn't even whimper or flinch when the needle pierced his tender skin. A blood sample was taken through the IV and sent to the lab with an order to rush the results. At this point, things began to slow down, at least enough for the nurse to speak to us about what was going on. She stated that the initial lab results requested by Willie's pediatrician found glucose in his urine. When I asked what that meant, she further explained that this caused a concern that Willie might have Type 1 Diabetes, a condition that, if left untreated, can be fatal. The nurse continued.

"But there is no way that he has Type 1 Diabetes, so you can relax."

"How can you be so sure," I asked.

"Because I have been an ER nurse here at Children's for more than 12 years and I have seen it all. The youngest diabetic that I have ever seen diagnosed was four years old and even that was unusual. Everything that we are doing right now is just precautionary, as if he were diabetic, to reduce the risk of long-term damage."

I immediately felt relieved. I understood that as a nurse at such a high-volume children's hospital, with so many years of experience had undoubtedly "seen it all." I took great comfort in her words, but when I looked down at Lora she still seemed distraught. As soon as the nurse left, I sat next to Lora and attempted to console her.

"Everything is going to be okay. The nurse even said that all of this was precautionary and that he doesn't have diabetes."

Lora just shook her head.

"You don't understand. He's not going to be okay and he does have diabetes."

"Why would you say that? We don't even have the lab results back yet and the nurse just said he doesn't have diabetes."

I felt like Lora was just being pessimistic. I was sure that Willie did not have diabetes, that he was just sick with the flu and would be fine. Lora responded.

"When my best friend, Danielle, was 11, she was diagnosed with Type 1 Diabetes. Willie has all the same symptoms that Danielle had and his breath even smells fruity."

Lora buried her face in her hands and sobbed. I was irritated that she thought she knew better than the nurse. Lora's comment about fruity breath reminded me that in our DUI training, we were taught that if we suspected a driver of being under the influence of alcohol, but their breath smelled fruity, they were most likely diabetic, which could be the cause for their impaired driving. But I still knew that Willie would be fine. Just to prove to Lora that Willie didn't have diabetes, I waited for the nurse to return.

"What else do you think could be wrong with Willie since he does not have diabetes?

"Well, I can't be sure, but the glucose in his urine is most likely an atypical symptom of the flu or a viral infection, which is really nothing to be too concerned with."

Exactly, I thought to myself. Two hours later, the lab results came back. The doctor walked in and confirmed that Lora's intuition had been correct. Willie was the youngest Type 1 Diabetic ever diagnosed up to that point at Children's Hospital and his blood sugar was over 600 milligrams per deciliter, which the doctor reiterated was life-threatening.

Lora and I were devastated. Even Willie seemingly sensed that something was very wrong and began screaming uncontrollably. Lora made preparations to breastfeed him in an effort to comfort him but was devastated again when the doctor told her that Willie could not have anything to eat or drink until they could lower his blood sugar over the next 24 hours. I had no idea what it meant to have Type 1 Diabetes, but I still refused to ask the doctor if Willie would be okay simply because I was unsure of the answer.

Willie was moved to the Neonatal Intensive Care Unit (NICU) where the nurses immediately started a saline drip and insulin drip. As they hooked Willie up to several different pumps, monitors and machines, I counted 14 tubes and wires coming out of his body. Through the entire night and into the next day, Willie never slept and he never stopped crying, with intermittent fits of screaming, each time until he had no strength left. Lora and I took turns laying in his bed and holding him in an attempt to comfort him but to no avail, Willie's pain and anguish lasted for what must have seemed like an eternity to a 10-month-old infant, that had no comprehension of what was happening, if his pain would ever end, or why his mother who at times was lying next to him refused to feed him.

While Lora cried alongside Willie through much of the night, I never shed a single tear. I refused. From the time I left the police department, my training had kicked in and I stayed on autopilot for the next three days. Lora and I never left his side throughout the entire ordeal and as Willie's blood sugar was stabilized, his symptoms seemingly vanished as if nothing had ever happened and he returned to his joyous, happy self, causing Lora and I to be overjoyed.

On Willie's last day in the NICU, it was not unusual to find him running, with the use of his walker, up and down the hallways laughing and bringing a smile to everyone he came into contact with. And while our little Willie was back, we had come to the realization that things would never be the same. We didn't fully comprehend or appreciate what it meant at the time, but Willie was now a chronically ill, insulin dependent, Type 1 Diabetic that had to count every single carbohydrate that went into his body and would for the rest of his life.

At that point, Willie was physically ready to leave the hospital, but Lora and I had no idea how to care for a child with Type 1 Diabetes. For this reason, on the fourth day, Willie was transferred from the NICU to the Children's Cancer Center because Willie's condition was not contagious, and neither were the children with cancer. Willie would now remain in the hospital as long as was necessary for Lora and I to learn to care for him and keep him alive on a daily basis.

That night, I sent Lora home to get some much-needed rest, and to check on our other two children who had been staying with family. As the sun set, it was as if the emotional wall that I had built up and the sun were connected. As darkness filled the room, with Willie sleeping on my chest, an uncontrollable dam of tears burst. I had never cried so many tears as I mourned the loss of my little Willie's health, a blessing that up to four days prior, I had taken for granted and, no matter what I did or didn't do, there was nothing I could do to fix it.

The training we received in the coming days taught Lora and I that we would solely be responsible for maintaining and sustaining Willie's life. We learned that Willie required a minimum of five shots per day and 10 to 12 finger sticks per day to maintain his blood sugar levels. The nurse explained that, while Type 1 Diabetes was a manageable disease, it required constant and vigilant care or, if left unchecked, could result in permanent brain damage or even death, especially for children under five years old. In order to avoid this, Lora and I would have to get up several times per night to maintain Willie's blood within the appropriate levels.

On day six, Lora and I took Willie home from the hospital, as we felt nervous, anxious and inadequate to provide the medical care he required to sustain life. For the next year, Lora and I took turns getting up every single night, multiple times per night to check and maintain Willie's blood sugar levels. We were grateful for the support of family and friends during that difficult time in our lives. However, there was no way anyone could have ever really understood the pressure put on us every day and especially every night, as we were aware that if we messed up, even once, it could have resulted in the permanent brain damage or death of our son.

As a direct result of Willie's diagnosis, I soon came to understand that leaving law enforcement, a career that I loved, was inevitable. I needed to be home nights and weekends to assist Lora with Willie's care. It wasn't fair to expect her to do it all on her own. I wasn't sure what I wanted to do or even what my options were but, fortunately, I already had a Bachelor's degree from Fresno State. The police chief worked with me during this difficult time and accommodated my schedule by allowing me to move into an administrative sergeant's role, which meant that I worked Monday through Friday from 8:00 a.m. to 5:00 p.m. It was a much-needed blessing at that time until Lora and I could figure out what our next step was.

Within a few short months of Willie's diagnosis, Lora and I left Willie, Clayton III and Jonah with their grandparents for a couple of hours to go out with friends and take a necessary break from diabetes. We decided to go bowling in an attempt to feel normal for a couple of hours. After arriving at the bowling alley, we were informed that if we were willing to wait 45 minutes, each game of bowling would be half price. We all agreed to go across the street to the bookstore. Throughout my life, anytime that I have walked into a bookstore or library, I have felt great power from the words of amazing authors like Alexandre Dumas,

Jane Austen, Samuel Clemens and so many others. However, simultaneously, I have often found it difficult to sift through the tens of thousands of books to find the greats.

On that particular evening, I walked up to the bestsellers and immediately noticed a book with a mysterious cover. I picked it up and observed mountains in the background and an obvious Andalusian influenced residence (keep in mind that my degree is in Geography) in the foreground covered in a dense fog. I read the title, *The Alchemist*. It was by an author I had never before heard of, Paulo Coelho. I turned the book over and read a quote on the back of the book: "Every few decades a book comes along that changes the lives of its readers forever." *Yeah right*, I thought to myself. But then I thought, *just what if...* I decided to purchase the book. Now, I had the difficult task of convincing Lora that I wanted to buy it. She knew better than anyone that I had a habit of buying books, reading the first couple of chapters, getting bored with them and tossing them aside. Nevertheless, I told Lora that I wanted to purchase *The Alchemist*. Lora simply took the book out of my hand and paid for the book herself. This was unprecedented *as if it was meant to be*, I thought.

The very next day I began reading *The Alchemist* and it was the first book in my life that I could not put down. I saw myself as Santiago and I understood that Santiago's difficult journey was a microcosm of my own life's journey.

When Santiago's life savings were stolen from him, it was no different from the loss that Lora and I experienced when Willie was diagnosed with Type 1 Dabetes. However, as I continued reading, Santiago's loss eventually provided him with so much more than he ever had before his life savings were taken. *How could this be possible*, I asked myself. *There is no way to take Diabetes from Willie*, I thought. While I still didn't have all the answers, as I finished the book, I remember having a distinct thought, *if I ever wrote a book, this is what I would write.*

Within months, the City Manager of the city I worked for retired. The police chief was promoted as the next City Manager and I was promoted to Assistant City Manager, which meant that my schedule was permanently changed so that Lora and I could, together, care for Willie. I decided to go back to school to obtain a Master's degree, but I was conflicted. I knew deep down that I wanted to nurture my desire and ability to write, to tell our story and to do it in such a way that others could relate to, without having to share the very deep and personal details of our diabetic experience. I just wasn't ready for that yet. The only problem was that I didn't even know if I had the skills necessary to become a writer. I applied to Pennsylvania State University's (Penn State) Master of Public Administration program because that's the line of work that I was already in and to the University of Mississippi's (Ole Miss) Master of Fine Arts

156

program in Creative Writing. Of course, as part of the application, Ole Miss required a writing sample.

I wrote the first two chapters of my first novel, entitled Iron Post Corner, and submitted my application. Within a few months, I received a phone call from a thoughtful professor at Ole Miss. I was so excited because I knew that he must have been calling to congratulate me on my acceptance. However, the professor explained that when he had applied to graduate school, he was not accepted to the first school he applied to and he was ready to quit. But when a professor from that university personally called him to tell him that his writing was amazing, they just didn't have room for him, he decided to continue the pursuit of his dreams, which eventually came true. The professor told me that the Creative Writing Department at Ole Miss had received over 120 applicants and they only were able to accept two, but that I was in the top five. He encouraged me to continue pursuing my writing career, yet when I was accepted into Penn State, I gratefully accepted and pursued a Master's degree in Public Administration.

As the years went by, I often thought of my unfinished novel. It was always in the back of my mind, gently nudging me to continue, but I never did. Then on April 1, 2014, our fourth son, Henry, was also diagnosed with Type 1 Diabetes at 20 months old while I was traveling out of state. Lora was amazing. She immediately recognized the signs and, as a result, was in and out of the hospital after an overnight stay. Because she recognized Henry's symptoms so early, his condition was never life-threatening, although Lora most certainly saved his life that day. While we were still saddened by Henry's diagnosis, our experience with Willie taught us that, as difficult as it was, we could do this.

Affectionately dubbed the Dynamic Duo, Willie and Henry are truly marvelous and incredible people. Willie is now nine years old and Henry is five. Willie's zest for life and infectious energy are admired and envied by everyone around him. Henry's passion for everything and everyone he loves is undeniable as he gives all of himself to everyone he comes in contact with. Those two boys have taught me, along with *The Alchemist's* Santiago, that sometimes our challenges in life are there to inspire us to rise above and to be more than we have become.

I can't explain how or why, but in October of 2015, I knew that it was time to finish *Iron Post Corner*— the novel that never would have been started had that series of events, beginning with Willie's diagnosis, not occurred. At first, I struggled to find the time to write, until I realized that the gift of time was provided each night that I woke up to check Willie and Henry's blood sugar but was unable to go back to sleep. It took two years to become a reality, but *Iron Post Corner* was published on November 22, 2017, and, while it immediately became an Amazon Bestseller, there is no doubt

158

in my mind that, just like Willie and Henry, *Iron Post Corner* has yet to realize its full potential. Regardless of what Iron Post Corner does or does not attain, it is a direct connection to our story as a family and the love, loss and redemption that we have experienced in this, our mortal sojourn.

Since Willie and Henry's diagnosis, Lora and I have become proficient in the care of Type 1 Diabetes. We can literally tell if our boys' blood sugar is high or low based on the color and consistency of their blood when we prick their finger before we even test for the actual blood sugar number. We also know, based on their mood, behavior and even the way their eyes look if they are high or low. We love all of our children and are so grateful for the literal miracle of modern medicine. Henry and Willie are every bit as lively and normal as anyone their age. Today they have the best medical equipment available and no longer need injections to receive the life-sustaining insulin that their bodies are unable to produce. They have insulin pumps that pump insulin into their bodies by wireless remote whenever they need it. They also wear continuous blood glucose monitors that monitor their blood sugar every three minutes through a wireless transmitter that limits their finger pokes to twice per day.

Willie and Henry have taught us so much, including that they can do anything, and I mean anything that anyone else can do. As difficult as it has been at times for Lora and I not to give in to diabetes, we actively choose to follow Willie and Henry's example to not let Type 1 Diabetes define who we are. While it is a real disease that affects us every day, Clayton III (17), Jonah (14), Heather (3), Lora and I stand with Henry and Willie and proclaim in the words of Dylan Thomas that we will "Rage, rage against the dying of the light [and we will]... not go gentle into that good night."

***

*Clayton Lucas is a sixth generation native of Oklahoma, where he currently lives and is serving as a City Manager. He has served in municipal government for more than 17 years, including as a police officer, firefighter and urban planner. Before earning a Bachelor's degree in Geography from Fresno State University and a Master's degree in Public Administration from Pennsylvania State University, Clayton lived in Venezuela for two years where he worked to serve others, learned to love the culture and people and became fluent in Spanish. He and his wife, Lora, have five children, Clayton III, Jonah, Willie, Henry, and Heather, two of which have Type 1 Diabetes. As a result, Clayton and Lora are advocates and supporters of the Juvenile Diabetes Research Foundation (JDRF) and any organization that furthers the efforts to find a cure for Type 1 Diabetes. He and his family love to travel internationally, participate in outdoor activities and spend time with family and friends. He has also written and published his debut novel, **Iron Post Corner,** an incredible, historical romance and compelling story of love, loss and redemption. For his book you can go to* www.ironpostcorner.com *or visit* www.claytonlucas.com.

ROAD TO REDEMPTION
James Yin

Most people are concerned about lifestyle. For my parents, strangers in a strange land, the focus had been on survival. They worked 365 days a year for over 30 years. They came to America with $600 and did the best with what they had to provide for my brother and I, but essentially we were most influenced by what we saw on TV, the music we listened to, and our bad friends.

While our parents were concentrating on the business side of things, they couldn't compete with society's influence on my life. In my quest of looking for my identity and a sense of belonging, I wound up finding those things in our inner-city gangs. Subconsciously I found it on the streets because I wasn't meeting my needs at home. It always starts off as fun and games until you're knee-deep. Life took me through a series of unfortunate events and that's how I ended up in prison.

But the real prison was in my mind. My parents did their best, but as a kid, I didn't understand that. All I could think was that my parents were trying to be controlling. On the one hand, I had my parents trying to put boundaries on me, and on the other I had my friends who just wanted to do what kids do.

The heroes and role models of my day were the pimps, players, and gangsters. I didn't have any positive influences or role models. When you're young you don't know any better. We thought that what we saw was cool and that we were supposed to do things because the other kids were doing it. We never thought about consequences. We were young, and parental rules pitted against the influence of my peers made the perfect recipe for rebellion. I got into trouble every year. I had been suspended from school, each year, since the third grade.

When I was nine years old I started drinking and experimenting with drugs. By twelve years old, I had joined my first gang. Looking back at the situation, I was trying to satisfy my need for love and significance. In my mind, the alternative to being home all day studying math and science was to go out, to get high, paid and laid. It was the type of life I saw my generation leading on television, in the music. It was all around me, it was enticing, but it was also destructive. I didn't feel at home or at school that I was allowed to express myself, so instead I did so in the most negative way possible.

Still, the streets taught me, heart. That was something you couldn't learn in school or at home. My parents did everything that they could think of to get me out of that life. They sent me to the number-one Catholic high school in New

York. They never thought that I would get admitted into the school, but I did. Once I was admitted, I wanted out. I totally rebelled and I did everything I could to make the school kick me out and continued doing what I knew best.

It got so bad that I was kicked out of four high schools in two years. My life began a downward spiral. I started running away from home, doing drugs and doing everything illegal under the sun. Even as a kid I'd always been a planner, so I had money on my mind and a retirement plan. I really thought that I was going to hustle hard and retire, but life had another plan for me. I was arrested. Then arrested again, and again, and again. I went from Spofford to Rikers Island to Upstate.

Sixteen was one of the worst year of my life. I was stabbed for my best friend then a month later I remanded for an unrelated charge. I did six months in jail and after I got out, some guys were sent from across the country to kill my boss and I took a bullet for him. You would think a person would learn their lesson, but I didn't. I felt like I had nine-lives.

That was the 1990s and Mayor Giuliani had come into office. There was a major crackdown in New York. Giuliani came after everyone. He went after organized crime and no one was safe. When Giuliani came in, most of my friends were either killed or arrested.

With my crew off the street, I began the next chapter in my life. There was an evolution from street gang, to organized crime, to doing my own thing. In my mind, at seventeen years old, I thought I had it all. I had money, cars, whatever I wanted. Nobody could tell me nothing. I was making more money than I knew what to do with- 10g's a week doing my own thing. Now with the gangs broken up, I was my own man.

Then things started to change. I got caught up. I lost everything I had hustled so hard for. I also learned what everyone already knows in their heart but doesn't want to admit. When you have everything, then everyone wants to be your friend, but when you have nothing... no one wants to know you. When I lost everything, I learned who was who. I also decided enough was enough, it was finally time to try to change my life.

Do What You Love

Having a record, I couldn't get hired by the city or state. This cut down my job prospects and made me hold tight to my money. It was at that time that I realized that I had a real problem with authority. There was no way that I could keep a normal 9 to 5 job. I would definitely have quit or been fired.

The only option I saw was to open my own business. I had heard the saying, "Do what you love and you will never work a day in your life." So, I opened a hobby store in Queens. It was what I loved, but it didn't do too well.

However, my entrepreneurial spirit came alive during this time. I was determined not to give up, so I was doing everything on my own without any help or experience. I thought that it would be better if I had partners than to go at it alone, so I invited my brother, my girlfriend and my brother's best friend to become partners with me.

What a mess.

That ended up being the worst business mistake I could have made, but it was a great learning experience. Together we bought a famous donut and ice cream franchise. As the weeks became months, I felt like a prisoner in my own store. Instead of owning a profitable business, I was working 80 hours a week. I didn't own a business, I bought myself a job. This was nothing like what I had imagined owning a business would be like.

And there was something else that I noticed during this time. No matter how much money I did or did not make, whether I was having a good week or a terrible one, each month I watched the landlord come with his hand out and get paid. Whether I made money or not, he did.

I talked with my mom about this and she supported me by buying a program for my birthday from Carleton Sheets, the bestselling author of the No Money Down® home study course. Carleton is the guy that most real estate gurus can point back to. His No Money Down program was probably the course they all bought to get started. He was a successful full-time investor and was teaching millions of people how to do creative real estate deals. He taught how to cash in on foreclosures, make profits with partners, earn profits in property management, and make money with real estate. The beauty of it was that I could do it in my spare time, I didn't need any experience, I didn't have to quit my job and I could have monthly cash flow.

Within six months of starting his program, I had my first three-family house with tenants. Having two tenants paid for my mortgage and I was also able to live in it rent-free. That's when I realized, "Holy s***, this s*** works!" I became so engrossed in real estate that I recognized that this was what I was passionate about. I decided that to get the best deals I needed to be in the real estate business. It sounds funny because nobody grows up saying they want to be an investor. But I'm so grateful that I found out that this was an option and that it became my passion.

The guy down the street from my store came in each day for donuts and coffee. One day he asked me if I wanted to get into real estate and I said, "Hells yeah!" As I began this new career I started finding great deals all day long, but I realized that it didn't matter what I found if I couldn't finance these deals. It was then that I decided to jump into financing mortgages. As it turned out, I loved it even better. In mortgages, I found my love of numbers. The reason that I loved them was because it's the numbers that tell the story.

While all of this was going on, my fiancée was pregnant with my daughter. Here I was working about 80 hours a week between the donut shop and doing real estate, but even putting in 80 hours a week, no money was coming in. It didn't make sense that I was working so hard that I never got to see my own house or spend time with my family, but that's what you work so hard for. What does it matter if you work so hard for your home and your family if you never get to see your house or see your family? I would come home late at night, hustling to make money to support us and getting hassled at home.

So, we decided to sell the business and I dove headlong into real estate. I envisioned real estate as my way out of the rat race. In my mind's eye I could see this coming to fruition, but not everyone shared my vision. In the beginning of a business, you don't know enough to make a deal happen. Couple that with working on commission. I would work all day and earn nothing. My fiancée just couldn't understand it. Her response was to ask, "Who works all day and doesn't bring home a paycheck?"

Finally, she said, "I'd respect you more if you worked for McDonald's." Her statement really cut me to the core. Everything in me was hoping that she would share this vision with me. I think that whoever your partner in life is, they should back you up. If you have your significant other on your side and you feel that positive encouragement, you can move mountains. After my daughter was born the relationship deteriorated to the point that we couldn't make it work and my fiancée left. That was the first time in my life that I had ever really had my heart broken. To counter that, I began to devote my time to my career.

Using all my free time to focus on my financial goals, my career finally began to flourish. I started to make some real money. I still have that first check from my first real estate deal, which I framed. It is for $10,845.00 and I framed it to remind me to never give up and that there is a light at the end of the tunnel. In just two short years I had accumulated 2 million dollars in assets and bought condos in Las Vegas and other popular areas. But the demons of my past kept catching up with me. As my success grew, so did my addictions.

I believed it was a loan officer's job to make money, party and drink, and I had mastered all three. One night when I was out drinking I got pulled over for DWI. With two firearms in my car, I landed in prison with a sentence of four and a half years. On top of everything going on in my own life, the real estate crash also happened at the same time and I lost everything. I lost my house. I lost my car. I even lost my dog. Most importantly, I lost my freedom. I had nothing left to take. It felt like God had stripped me bare-naked to my soul.

In the prison environment, I had a lot of time to

reflect. One thing that became very apparent was there were people in prison who could spend twenty years in there and say it was a short time, and there were others who would spend a week inside and say it felt like an eternity. It had everything do with how they viewed it. It was all about perspective. Whatever mindset the person had, would determine how their time inside felt. Once I saw that it was all about perception, I saw the opportunity to turn this tragedy into triumph!

The first thing I learned in prison that changed my thinking was that time is a gift. On the outside, there are so many demands: social, economic, and family demands. Everyone is fighting for your time to the point that you feel like you don't have any time at all. But time is our most valuable gift, and now I had plenty of it. What could I do with all the time behind bars that I now saw as a gift? I chose to work on my mind, body, and spirit. Those were the most important qualities in life and those were the exact ones that I had neglected to attain while growing up. Those are also the qualities that most people don't spend enough of their time developing. Instead, in life, we chase the almighty dollar and end up chasing our own tails.

Determined to make the best use of my time while incarcerated, I started reading. Soon I was reading all types of subjects, from spiritual books to law books. I couldn't get enough. It was like my brain had been starving and now I had a feast in front of me. While I was stuck in prison I read over 600 books on business, finance, and self-development. I got my diploma as a paralegal, specializing in real estate law. I even got a job in the prison's law library.

When I was in jail I was learning the law and I learned the word "chattel." Chattel means movable property. As a prisoner, the legal term referred to us as movable personal property, as chattel. Having success before I went to jail and losing everything while I was in there made me feel even more like State property and less like a human being. I had to turn all this tragedy into triumph. My theory was that I needed to understand the rules of the game. If I didn't understand the rules of the game, how could I play?

I also took this time to get into shape. I was bench pressing 365 pounds and feeling great physically. Looking back at it, this was the most important thing that could have happened to me. In one of my darkest times I picked up this Buddhist book. I read that all suffering comes from aggravated clinging. What that really meant is that if you someone, or a possession, that the thought of it, the desire and the attachment. That's where the suffering comes from. This also applied to the people in our lives that we have lost. That's when I decided to let everything go. How many people walk around wounded, carrying their past hurts like a big heavy bag of weights? I decided to drop that bag! I couldn't let my past weigh me down or define me. This was my last chance. I had to take it and make the most of it because the alternative was death. I felt like I had used all the lives I had been offered; like I was in a video game with no more lives left.

With all that time, I was able to reflect on how I almost died three times. My close friends lost their lives and yet here I was. God had given me many chances and these friends had died tragically. Why them and not me? The only conclusion I could come up with was that God had a divine plan for me, I had to do something good with my life. After accepting that my life had a purpose bigger than myself, I started receiving waves of inspiration. Because I was living in limbo and the world was moving on without me, the only thing I could really do was look forward, make plans and prepare for the inevitable things in life and what I was going to make happen. I took out a sheet of paper and started writing. Creating on paper exactly the life I wanted. Anything I didn't know how to do and wanted to accomplish, I went to the library and researched how. I developed a blueprint for my own life based on everything I had learned. I created a body of work with over 1,000 pages detailing everything I wanted and how to achieve each goal.

I left prison feeling confident about my game plan and I had focus and clarity on what I wanted to accomplish. I decided that it was time to stop wasting time and get down to business. It was a challenge, but I did it. It felt like an evolution. I was able to apply the street smarts I gained on the outside with the book smarts I had learned on the inside.

Three years ago, I began to buckle down and started going all at it. The second year of going all in, I freed myself financially. I finally had freedom and the world was now mine. Once I was able to buy back my time, which is our most valuable resource, I was finally able to work more fully on my life's mission. I began to think about what my purpose was and what my contribution would be. I wanted to leave behind something much bigger than me. By this time, I had created four successful companies.

Now I am working on leaving a legacy. I am creating a trust for future generations of my family. Now I realize what life after death is. In so many ways I figuratively died and was reborn. Now I know that I want to create something bigger than me. Something that I can leave behind, a legacy. I want to develop a trust that will enable my daughter and future descendants to have options in life. I don't want them to have to work if they have something better and bigger to do. My goal is not for them to be entitled, but to contribute their God-given talent to the world. I will have two provisions for the trust. First, they have to go to school for the rest of their lives. Benjamin Franklin said the best investment is in your education. The second thing they have to do is donate time and talents to the foundation I built so that it will keep it in a perpetual state.

I don't care what they're going to school for. If they want to sing, dance, paint. I just want each of them to go to keep learning, to discover & develop their God given talents, and use them to better this world. God gives everybody a talent; you just have to go find it. The second part is that they have to donate time to the foundation.

I've got two important causes that I'd like to dedicate my life to. One is teaching high school kids fiscal literacy. We spend our whole life in school learning about things that have no practical use and things that we will never use again, but no one teaches us about managing our finances. We will handle money every day of our lives and yet this is not covered at all. I feel that if we can catch kids in high school and teach them to be fiscally literate then that can be the turning point for them. We have to make it exciting and applicable. If we can get their attention before they reach out for bad influences or get-rich-quick schemes, it could make all the difference to their quality of life. Most kids are concerned about cars, kids, and money. If they had a roadmap then they wouldn't have to find negative ways to make money.

The other goal of my foundation is helping senior citizens manage their golden years. They are large in numbers, but many of them have been forgotten, and sadly have also forgotten how to dream. They're like, "I'm retired, now what?" They worked their whole lives to retire, and now they wonder if this all there is. As they were working and saving they had big goals and plans in mind. Now that they have retired, their priority isn't doing what they always wanted to do, it's trying to live off what they saved. They have forgotten how to dream and there are so many sad endings.

Watching the History Channel, I saw 74-year-old women who are flying fighter jets and driving race cars. There are happy and productive senior citizens, and that's what we should plan for in our life after we reach our pinnacle. We need new role models at every stage of our life. People just need help to break down their financial situation, prepare for the future and plan to reach their goals that they still have yet to accomplish. I want to create a program for making happy and successful senior citizens, who plan well for what is to come.

Today I am grateful to have an amazing relationship with my daughter. My life is on-track and my business is growing at an incredible pace. I've also met so many great people and mentors along the way who have helped inspire me and chart my own path. The key to building lasting business relationships is being interested in what the other party has to say and creating value. We each are passionate about something, and when you find someone who shares your passion or is passionate about something you would like to learn, you find that there is so much to build a relationship on.

Business is better than ever. One of my companies that I built is now on Wall Street, Brick Equity LLC. (Brick Equity is a comprehensive finance solution for businesses. We help owners build a business credit profile, secure money for their business and we even score businesses, so they can be approved for additional financing. Basically, it's the type of company that I would have wanted to work with when I was building a business.)

When my parents came to America in 1974, I'm sure that they had a different view of how life in the US would be. But this is the path I've walked, and I am grateful for their support. We each have learned a great deal about life and I want to thank them for never giving up on me. Mom, dad, I love you. To my daughter, you make me want to be a better man. I will always be there for you. Thank you for being my inspiration. I also want you and others to know that through all of this, I have learned that going through your own challenges can make you into a better person.

Tony Robbins said, "We ask why our lives can't be easy? However, God isn't concerned about our convenience, he's concerned about our character." The true gifts of God are our setbacks; they are here to shape us, strengthen us and forge us. To help us grow as human beings. I know for me they are exactly what made me who I am and I am grateful for each hard experience I made my way through. My life's motto now is to be grateful for where I came from and also where I am headed. This journey has been a spiritual one and I'm excited to see what the future holds for me and my mission.

People ask, "How does the son of immigrant parents end up going from the mean streets to Wall Street, live the American dream, and end up achieving success in New York City?" Answering that question is my motivation for sharing my story here. I want to inspire people with my own life because I know what the alternative is. There are people who love you and depend on you.

In the beginning, it feels like everyone around you is succeeding and you're the only one who is failing. I know because I've been from rags to riches, to rags to riches. By reading my story I think that people can see that if I can do it, s*** they can overcome any challenge in life. Most importantly they can see how to take their tragedies and turn them into triumph.

***

James Yin is an Author, Speaker, Trainer, and Successful Real Estate Investor. He has gone from the mean streets to Wall Street. He is the son of hard-working, first-generation Americans. He says he was educated in the School of Hard Knocks to become a successful real estate investor and Chief Executive Officer of Brick Equity, which helps small businesses and investors find additional funding. He lives in Brooklyn, New York. When attending a workshop taught by James, you'll learn great insight and wisdom on how to get capital for your business to help ensure faster growth and build your dreams. www.brickequity.us

YOU'RE GOING TO FLY NOW

Nathan Tea

Listen, no one ever said life would be easy or fair. Take it from a guy who's been through 16 years of extremes on both ends of the spectrum. I've already been through everything from losing loved ones, to bullying, to divorced parents, losing animals, moving multiple times, growing up in an overly sensitive country and almost losing my little sister. Today I feel like I am on top of the world. Though it didn't start out this way for sure. I count my blessings often because after years of trying to figure things out I decided to take control of my situation.

Today I feel like I'm on top of the world. I am well respected and have a good paying job. I am also a policy maker as a Nevada Youth Legislator. I have great relationships with my teachers and administrators at school, I have an amazing mom and sister, my family, mentors, tons of friends, and I know I am on the right track in life. I am also a flight student.

I remember the first time my instructor had me take over the yoke, he looked at me and said, "You're going to fly now." My palms were sweating, but I knew that I could do this since it wasn't even close to the hardest thing I had ever done (I kept spinning around on the ground and couldn't figure out how to take off, but then I got focused and finally made a successful takeoff and landing).

The hardest thing I have ever done was having to grow up without a permanent father figure in my life. When I was still a little kid my mom and dad went through a nasty divorce that left my mom with next to nothing. We struggled for a few years because she left her high paying executive job to start a business that would allow her to work around my sister and I, while working mostly from home. We saw my father occasionally on the weekends, but he was rarely present with us even if he was at the house. I felt like I was growing up without someone to teach me how to be a man. My father wasn't the kind of person who helped with homework, taught about responsibilities, money, or there to give advice on how to act or how to deal with certain situations. Me being my mom's first born and 'the young man of the house' I wound up having to figure out how to grow from a boy to a man for myself. This forced me to re-prioritize my goals and dreams when additional responsibilities were added. I also had to learn how to survive on my own in the world.

At the age of 15 I had to start planning for how to get myself to college. I needed to learn how to drive, get a license, and get a job to pay for it all. Somehow, I managed to pull it all together as I turned 16 when my mom made a deal with some long-time family friends which landed me a truck and a good paying job with a large company, that really cared about my wellbeing. I also received an opportunity to start a very prestigious political position at the same time I was starting my college search.

Loneliness is one of the hardships that I have struggled through since I was a young boy. Even though I had my mom and little sister around when I wasn't at my father's house. Through most of my childhood I was trying to find a place where I felt comfortable. It was hard for me because I felt like there wasn't anyone who I could trust my problems to, so I kept the weight of what I was going through on my shoulders alone. Every time I went to my dad for help he would be preoccupied by other things, as my sister and I were never his priority. One of the coping mechanisms I turned to was videogames, and that is all I would do while I was at his house. What pulled me out of the darkness were the new friends that I made in 8th grade, and from then I kept finding some more amazing friends, and my mom who showed me the light of the world and helped pull me from the shell I had built around myself. They brought me into Mixed Martial Arts as a stress release, and I've found some amazing mentors who give me advice on any aspect of my life that they can.

In hindsight, it seems like I had no apparent path, or any desire to achieve anything other than just escaping into those games. This is the path of someone who doesn't want success, or doesn't know what it looks like. Instead the person locks themselves away and hides from their problems. That is what I did for a good chunk of my childhood. I still regret not going outside finding new friends on the weekends and doing the kind of things any kid should do. I should have stayed outside until dark exploring and having fun. Rode my bike and played in the dirt like my mom said they did as kids. All the things that I should have done, I didn't do. I wasn't that kind of kid. Now I'm making up for lost time.

My mom kept us busy and never let me play videogames or watch TV at her house, so I made up for lost time at my dad's house. That is not the life I wanted, but it was the life that I chose. Everything is a choice, you choose to eat pizza, you choose where you are going, you choose who you are going to date, or marry, you choose your life path with every step you take. These are all important decisions (well maybe not the pizza.) They have the power to affect your entire life, and each small choice is going to be greatly impactful in the future for better or worse. It just depends on if you made the right choice. Now let's get into the good stuff. What follows are seven methods that I have used to get me through the numerous hard times in my life:

"A leader has eyes that see, the follower is blind."- Jennifer Baker

1. Persistence, knowing how and when to push yourself to the other side.

When life knocks you down you've got to get right back up. Don't let yourself get beaten because you think you're too weak or it's too hard. Because you are STRONG, and nothing is too HARD. The harder you push to achieve success, the more life will throw at you, testing to see if you are WORTHY of receiving SUCCESS.

Those that aren't worthy are the ones who GIVE UP, the ones who say, "I'm too WEAK," or, "It's too HARD." To those of you who have said that, you have already FAILED. You will NEVER reach success without an I CAN DO THIS attitude. It is possible to change your current mindset to an "I can do this" mindset, but you must be willing to embrace the path ahead because it will be brutal, you will feel pain and you will have a surplus of stress. Enjoy these things and the lessons that you will learn from them and know it will all be worth it in the end.

It's the same with many things in life. You must use persistence in order to complete anything. Especially in working out. With workouts, you must do it consistently in order to achieve any results. Without persistence, there will not be any results and you won't get stronger. It may seem easier to stop or quit but you need to stick with the grind no matter what because if you cheat the grind, it will drop you and it will hurt. Then you are back at ground zero, the beginning, where you have to restart everything and work your way back to the top. That is why it's actually easier to stay in motion and to keep persisting. Hence Newtons law of motion, an object in motion will stay in motion, unless an external force acts upon it and the same applies to an object at rest.

When you are in the final stretch of your life, do you want to say to yourself, "That was easy?" Or do you want to say, "Holy crap, what a ride this was." It is entirely your choice. Live risk-free and unsuccessful or take many risks and get knocked down and get back up again and again, but in the end, achieve true success and everlasting happiness with no regrets of what you should have done. The choice is all yours, so make it!

"Let me tell you something you already know. The world ain't all sunshine and rainbows. It is a very mean and nasty place and it will beat you to your knees and keep you there permanently if you let it. You, me, or nobody is gonna hit as hard as life."- Rocky Balboa

2. Knowing everything is temporary. Nothing lasts forever.

If there is anything I've learned in life, it is that nothing lasts forever, because if things lasted forever, then there wouldn't be any room for anything new or better. This is one of life's basic laws. Like the old saying goes, "Out

183

with the old and in with the new." I had a friend since first grade, and she and I were best friends until about freshman year of high school, at which point she and I started dating. I thought that she was the love of my life, but after two short years we broke up and haven't spoken very much since. I was heartbroken for a couple of days, but then I remembered something, and that simple tho*ught was, this was all part of my life's greater plan. My life now is nothing like the life I will be able to create in the future, and if I was supposed to be with this person then I would be.*

I've moved so many times in my life that I can't even remember most of the names of people that I went to school with. The point of my saying NOTHING LASTS FOREVER is to show you that no matter what comes your way, there will always be an end to it. Whether it is within a week or several months to even years, it will always end.

Take the Ebola virus, for example. It originated in Africa and lasted from 2014 to 2016. During that time, it claimed the lives of some eleven thousand people within Sierra Leone, Liberia, and Guinea. Now the deadliest disease of 2014 is curable. It didn't last forever nor will anything organic or not in this entire universe.

Or another example, Hurricane Katrina. This was originally just a tropical storm but was upgraded to a Class 5 Hurricane. The one thing that made this storm so terrible was its destructive power, but it still came to an end. If this isn't enough proof to show you that nothing lasts forever, take a look at nature. Go look up any natural phenomena. There is a natural cycle of life, and that cycle is, "start, Growth, and finish." All matter follows these three basic stages of the life cycle.

Everything, no matter what it is, will end eventually. This being said, your struggles will be prolonged, they will be numerous, and they will all be difficult in some way. However, just remember that as long as you keep trying you will make it through. These trials will end. Just keep persisting and you will make it to the other side of the storm.

3. Grounded by faith and knowing it is as sure as gravity.

Keep what you believe in close to your heart and make that the part of your life that keeps you in check. During the times where I felt like there was nothing left for me, I kept one thing close to my heart, and that was my belief that there was a greater power in this universe and, I was to do its bidding, live my life through the struggles it threw at me, and persevere through them. That is the main thing that kept me going through those hard times.

Too many people allow their beliefs to be suppressed because it is out of the norm. To that I say don't listen to the suppressors, follow your beliefs and they will not lead you astray. Keep what you believe in close to heart and use it as a compass in all of your decisions. That way you won't ever make the wrong decision.

During my times of hardship, keeping true to my faith is what helped me make the right decisions to help me push on through, keeping me focused on what was important and not being led astray. I think if I didn't keep my faith close, that my life would be very different today.

What if Aristotle didn't fight against the popular belief of Copernicus, That the earth was the center of the universe, but in fact it was the sun? What would life be like today if he didn't stick true to his faith? The reason why modern astronomy has come so far is that it started with one person. A philosopher named Aristotle who believed that the earth was just a planet rotating around a giant ball of gas that we call the sun. At the beginning when he first released his findings, no one believed him. They called him a hypocrite and a liar because it was against the popular belief that the earth was the center of the solar system and the sun rotated around it. Alas, Aristotle held true, even through all the criticism, and he finally proved to everyone that the earth was not the center of the universe, but in fact it was the sun. Just remember that your beliefs do not need to be popular to be true.

4. Find like-minded people/mentors who you can talk to.

One of the things that I would greatly recommend to you is to find people who think like you but are wiser and surround yourself with them. That energy will fill your mind and body and help you through whatever it is that you are going through. These people can be there for you when you need advice on anything you might have a question about, or they can help you through any trouble. A couple of years ago my main mentors were my mom, my counselor, my leader at church, and some of my closest friends. I felt like I could go and talk to them about anything, and with their help, I made it through my loneliness.

Some of the most successful people in the world have used like-minded people to help them get to where they are by taking advice and tips from them.

I cannot stress to you how imperative it is to have wiser like-minded people surrounding you because most of the time they could know something that you don't. They will have the answers to a question that you may not. Many famous people from the past have had mentors or like-minded people there coaching them throughout their entire lives.

I'm going to take a fictional person, for example, Rocky Balboa from the Rocky series created and played by Sylvester Stallone. In the movie series he started off as just some guy from a lower income city and he wanted to box because that was all he was good at. So he joined a gym and the owner of the gym started training him and mentored him throughout the beginning of his career. By the final movie, Rocky wound up mentoring the son of his first rival just the same way he was mentored.

5. There are no shortcuts in life.

Look, there aren't any shortcuts in life that will lead you to a rewarding outcome. Those exist for the people that don't want to take any risks. However, like in any other case of trial and tribulation, the easy route will not reward you as much as the hard route will. As once quoted by Beverly Sills, "There are no shortcuts to anyplace worth going."

The simple fact of life is that there are no shortcuts, and if there are, those that take them will always fail. Trust me if there were any shortcuts in life, people like the Pope, Dalai Lama, Mahatma Gandhi, Og Mandino or Jack Canfield would've found them already. The accomplishments of the big-time authors and motivational speakers, and leaders is plenty of proof that there aren't any shortcuts to anything worth having. You must set lofty goals and then go to work so that you can attain them.

6. Always tell yourself, YOU CAN DO IT!

Always remember to keep your head up and march onward to bring yourself success in every aspect of your life. Telling yourself, "you can do it" can be very beneficial. If you tell yourself that every day, eventually you'll get it in your head that you can actually do it. Then, you will always remember that you can achieve anything you set your mind to moving forward. This is called self-motivation. It's a rather easy concept to understand once you figure it out. Just repeat something over and over to yourself looking in the mirror and eventually your brain hears it so much it becomes ingrained. This being said, I challenge you to look at yourself every morning in the mirror and tell yourself, "I can do_____."

7. Take the time to think about your situation from a 30,000-foot view.

Something very important my mom told me once was if you're in a snag, take a step back and take a look at what you have going for you from a 30,000-foot view because usually that will give you a better perspective on what lies ahead. Now that I am taking flying lessons I absolutely know that this is true.

I've included this method to show you that even in the hard times. With all of the other methods I've given you, sometimes it's very easy to overlook something and thus you need to take a step back and check out what you have going for you in life. Count your blessings, gifts and talents.

When I was still in elementary school, I felt that I had no one that liked me. I felt alone, but my mom told me to take a step back and look at what I did have. Once I started counting my blessings, I realized that I wasn't alone. I had a lot of people around me who cared for me and wanted the best for me, and I had plenty of good things going for me. I was told again and again that I was blessed because I was handsome, I could often be charismatic whenever I broke out of my shell, and I had a great   family that only wanted the best for me.

In closing, I'd like to end my chapter in this amazing book by saying thank you for the amazing opportunity to co-author this book with incredible people, and the best publisher I could have asked for.

To you the reader my wish for you is to have the opportunity to achieve true success and everlasting fulfilling happiness. That is all I want for everyone. It has been both painful and a blast to write this chapter about myself, the struggles I've been through, and the tools that I've used to get through them.

***

Nathan Tea is a phenomenal young man who has overcome a great deal. Currently he is a Nevada Youth Legislator, professional speaker, author, healthy community and anti-bullying advocate, Future Business Leaders of America member, and youth empowerment advocate. Nathan is a paid intern for a major international company, is proficient with technology and helps run large and small events for Success GPS and for local government officials. He is also a pilot in training. Nathan is working on contributing to his next books with his mom and sister in the LAUNCH YOURSELF Series and is excited to see where the future leads.

OVERCOMING OBSTACLES
Jim Wheeler

You know, it's kind of weird. I've never really thought of myself as a greatly successful person. Which is why I was truly surprised when I was asked to contribute to this book. I've always just done what needs to be done and never really dwelled on the past or the obstacles thrown in my way. Although upon reflection, I guess I have made some amazing accomplishment in my life. Successful businessman, CEO, Nevada State Assemblyman, Majority Whip and then Minority Leader. But most of all, all three of my children are successful in their own way. That's probably my greatest achievement. But this book is about obstacles, and looking back, there have been many. The greatest of which was mental. I'll explain.

My father had a terrible disease for most of his life that in my early years was not considered a disease, but instead a social problem. He was an alcoholic. Now don't get me wrong, he was never abusive or anything that most associate with alcoholism, but the effects on my sister's and my life were far reaching. When I was only 2 and my sister was 4, my dad got in a car accident while under the influence that took the life of our mother and broke his back, leaving us two small children with no one to care for us. Originally, we were taken in by a great aunt and uncle on our mom's side who at the time were in their late 50s. From what I understand this was supposed to be a temporary arrangement until my dad could get back on his feet. But as it turned out, he never really did.

Dad was one of the smartest men I have ever known. He was in the automotive business and always held an executive position within every company I can remember him working for. He was Vice President of STP Corp, VP at Shelby Motors, VP at TuneUp Masters, and President of another successful company in the automotive world. He was a great businessman and made his employers copious amounts of money with his business and marketing knowledge, but he never got over his alcoholism and couldn't really hold a job. So, as it turns out, we ended up living most of our young lives with our Aunt Olive and Uncle Dave.

At the time of the accident, Olive and Dave lived on a small ranch in Southern California that was really too small to provide a living, so they both worked outside as well. Olive had gotten a job at Lockheed Burbank as a "Rosie the Riveter" during WWII and kept that job even after the war and all the way to her retirement in the late 70s. Dave had a small automotive repair shop in Burbank and would work long hours there and at the ranch. Being products of the great depression, they worked very hard and saved every penny they could, finally reaching a point in life where they were financially stable.

I'm sure when my sister and I came into their lives we upset the whole applecart, and as we were told for most of our young lives, absolutely ruined their later years. But in those days family took care of each other and no one depended on the government for their family's upbringing or care.

While they were definitely not rich, my aunt and uncle were financially stable and were able to provide us with a good middle-class life. We had our own home in a nice neighborhood, took vacations to Tahoe every year, attended a private catholic school during our elementary years and did most of the things that any other middle-class kids would do. Some would say that we had a lot more advantages than most... and they would be right.

However, there was always the behind the scenes, behind the closed doors machinations that I'm sure a lot of families go through and never make it to the light of day. I'm not talking about physical abuse, although there were plenty of butt-whippings and even some thumpings. "Spare the rod, spoil the child" was taken quite literally in our house. What I'm talking about is unintended mental abuse that carries on into our later years and which some people never really get over.

For as long as I can remember, I was told by those who raised us, those who we were supposed to look up to, those whose words meant everything, that I was worthless. I was a burden. And the absolute best one, the one I always remember, that I would never amount to anything.

It all started out with "You're just like your father. You'll never amount to anything" whenever they were mad at me. Then, of course, if my sister or I did something wrong, they would make sure we knew that they were right all along, we would never amount to anything. How could a child be as stupid as we were? This was the narrative we grew up with and heard all the time. Eventually, I think we started to believe it ourselves, causing a lot of bad feelings about ourselves, and whenever anything went wrong giving ourselves justification for failure that followed into our adult lives.

My sister, who had it even worse than I did, overcame it a little earlier. She was, and is, pretty tough. She worked her way through school and went on to achieve a Master's in education and became a teacher, a position she retired from some 30 years later. She is, and always has been my rock. She was the only one I could really talk to in my early years as she was the only one who knew exactly what was happening inside our home. While we obviously didn't know that we were going through something that children shouldn't be subjected to, we also had no idea that we were any different than anyone else. Please don't get me wrong. She has had problems in her life, but seemed to be able to focus on her goals a little earlier than I was able to.

I bounced around and continued to fail. After all, I knew I'd never amount to anything anyway. I would come from my home in California as a teenager to work on ranches in the Carson Valley of Northern Nevada as a summer job or work for one of my dad's business acquaintances in the automotive field. All the while with no real direction or goal in mind except one. I always wanted to live in the Carson Valley area, as I thought it was the most beautiful place on earth. I just had no idea or plan how I was going to accomplish this goal.

I got married at an early age and went to work after dropping out of college. When my wife got pregnant two years later with my baby girl Dana, I decided to join the Air Force in the waning years of the Vietnam era. Thankfully, I was stationed in Altus, Oklahoma for most of my tour. When the baby came the pressures of a new family were probably too much for us and we divorced shortly thereafter. Looking back now I realize that I had no earthly idea how to raise a child. To me, all love was tough-love. After all, that's all I can remember from my childhood. It must be the proper way to do things. However, with a baby there is no such thing as tough-love. They're little, helpless, and depend on you for everything in their lives. The hardest and most conflicting part was the love I felt for that child was in complete odds with everything I knew about raising a child based on my own experiences.

After the divorce and leaving the Air Force I went back home and looked for work. I bounced from job to job, got remarried and eventually got a great job on the police force. That's when things slowly began to change for me.

I learned through my experiences that maybe I wasn't such a bad guy after all. I was actually pretty good at what I did and was able to help people along the way. The mental change was slow, but looking back now, I think that the team building and "I can" attitude of the military really helped me. It wasn't like I just woke up one day and everything changed. It was more of a slow realization that I *was* a good person, that I *would* amount to something and that yes, in many ways, I was just like my dad. After all, as I said before, Dad was one of the smartest people I ever met, so being like him in some ways was a *good* thing.

My confidence level seemed to grow, little by little, every day. Even though I had a good job, I decided that I really wanted more. My son Nick, and daughter Charlee were then in the picture and it just felt like I had to do something that would leave a legacy for my kids. Then I remembered: I was once talking to my godfather who told me, "You can have any title in business you want, but only one will ever matter. That title is owner." I decided right then and there that I would take a chance and build something that my kids would be proud of.

Having grown up in two different and divergent worlds due to my love of ranching and rodeo as a hobby and my connections in the automotive business due to my dad, I had a couple of choices to draw on for my own company. I decided on the automotive business. Why? Simple, I knew it better. I was always into fast cars and the parts and mechanics that made them go faster and it seemed whenever I needed a job I would always revert to that business. Also, building a new ranch was way too expensive to take on with a young family. That's when we started our company.

My dad and I had an idea how to make a centrifugal supercharger that would fit under the hood of most production vehicles and be quiet, reliable, and dependable while adding 40% more horsepower all at the same time, so we started out designing it and building a prototype. I mortgaged my house and we lived very simply for a couple of years while we were in the process of making our first prototype. I also contracted myself out to some aftermarket companies getting their products smog legal through the California Air Resources Board to make a few extra bucks as I was the only one at the time who knew how to get some of these parts exempted through the board.

We borrowed a '90 Mustang from a friend that owned a Ford dealership and set about installing the supercharger and performing some minor testing. Once we were done we thought, what now? How do we get this product to market given my lack of funds? I think that's where this story really connects to the overcoming obstacles theme of this book. I had a crazy idea.

Once the supercharger was installed, my wife and I packed up the Mustang and set out from our home in California to Michigan. Why Michigan? That's where Ford Motor Company has their main offices. In a true "go big or go home" moment I figured we had nothing to lose.

We took our time getting there, making sure the supercharger worked well and met or exceeded our expectations. We even took the long way around, adding a few days to the trip just to make sure. Once we were in Dearborn, the home of Ford, I drove the car to the headquarters of Ford Motorsports and waited in the parking lot. When I saw the head of that division come out, I called him over and showed him the supercharger and installation and asked if he would like to drive it. Being a good "gearhead," I suspected that he would not be able to turn down a ride. I was right.

After he drove the car around Dearborn we went back to the Motorsports office and he invited me inside. We discussed the pricing and I was pleasantly surprised when he asked if we could make it with the Ford logo as a private label part instead of under the Powerdyne name.

Obviously, I said yes. I left Michigan with a purchase order from one of the biggest companies in the automotive business for 100 superchargers, at around $2,000 each as an initial order. Do you think I could have done that without confidence in my abilities and confidence in myself? Looking back now, I think that was the truly defining moment when I completely overcame the largest mental obstacle in my life and realized there was nothing I couldn't do.

The rest is pretty much history. I returned to California, went directly to the bank and borrowed enough money to get the company started on the strength of that one purchase order. In the months that followed, we made deals with many other companies to both private label the supercharger and with others to sell it under the Powerdyne name. We never stopped growing that company right up to the time I sold my interest in it.

During this time, I was able to realize my goal of living in the Carson Valley area of Northern Nevada and eventually retired there at an early age. But being me, I couldn't stay still for long. One day I was sitting on the couch and was yelling at some politician on the TV when I decided maybe I should do something about it instead of just voicing my complaints. A few days later, I was talking to then Congressman Dean Heller about a project I had in mind when he stopped me and asked, "Why aren't you in politics?" I laughed and said, "That's the last thing I want to do." To which he replied that that was exactly why I should get into it. We needed people who didn't see it as a career and wanted to help change things for the better. To be honest, I didn't think much of it at the time.

A few days later I was talking to then Assemblyman James Settelmeyer who told me he was not running for the Assembly again and instead would be running for the open Senate seat in our district, leaving his Assembly seat open. I ran for that seat, was defeated in a 4-way primary and ran again in the next session and won. I have been the Assemblyman for Nevada District 39 since, and was named Majority Whip in the 2015 session, Deputy Minority Leader in the 2017 session, and soon after the session was named Minority Leader going forward into the 2019 session.

I guess what I mean to say here is that you can overcome any obstacle in your way. The biggest of which are mental. I don't believe I ever would have had the success I have had if I still felt the sense of self-doubt that permeated my youth. When dealing with other people, one of the things that comes across in those first impressions are your feelings of confidence in yourself and your mission. It doesn't matter how many people say you can't do something as long as you believe in yourself. As Henry Ford once said, "Whether you think you can or you think you can't, you're right!"

***

Jim Wheeler is a successful businessman and politician from the state of Nevada. A member of the Republican Party, he was founder and CEO of Powerdyne Automotive Products, is an Assemblyman for the 39th District and is currently serving as House Minority Leader. He also served in the United States Air Force. He is a true believer in fiscal responsibility and minimal government and takes very seriously representing those he serves and isn't afraid to face anything head on.

PROPELLED BY LOVE

Craig Nielson

At the age of 21, I fell into an extreme depression. I was so severely depressed that I reached a point where I could no longer function or care for myself, and as a result, I was hospitalized for three weeks. This was the turning point in my life. This was the point in my life where I began to actually *live*. Everything I am and everything I've experienced today grew out of that experience.

I am now twenty-five plus years removed from that experience and when I look back to that time in my life and see all that my life experience has become from then to now, I am in awe. Back then if you had told me twenty-five years from now I would have the life I do today, I would have told you that would never be possible. I'm in awe at how much joy I have experienced. I'm in awe of the amount of love I have received, and I am in awe of the vast richness that has filled my life. My life today is one that back then would never have been conceivable to me.

The feeling of powerlessness and hopelessness was overwhelming. Fear was all consuming. I wasn't suicidal but wanted to die. Looking back, the reality was I just wanted to stop feeling what I was feeling. It made sense that death would put an end to that feeling. Now I can see that it wasn't so much that I wanted to stop living, but I wanted to stop living... like *that* anymore.

My heart breaks today when I hear of the tragedy of suicides. I'm heartbroken by the thought that another life has been destroyed by that terrible feeling. But I get it. I can't speak for those who have taken their own life. I cast no judgment on those who have. I don't know what *their* experience was. I do know what it's like to feel completely worthless, hopeless, scared, and alone and in a state of complete despair. I know what it is like to want that feeling to end.

My heart breaks from knowing my experience and in knowing that from that very dark place in my life, I grew out of it. It didn't last forever. I recovered. My life has become full, and today I can say that I am truly happy. My heart aches and I pray for those who for reasons I'll never know, never found their way out of darkness.

This is why I've decided to share my story, my knowledge, and my inspiration. Until recently, I never openly shared this part of my life with others outside my immediate family and a few close friends. Mostly because I was afraid of what others would think. The stigma that is associated with depression also contributed to me hiding my story.

I kept this story to myself until years later in response to what I see as a growing epidemic of people simply medicating themselves for depression because of the belief that it's just the way they are and therefore, they have no control over it. I've also come to recognize that there is an epidemic of low self-worth in the world today which has to lead to much abuse and neglect of others, and to me is the root of evil.

An essential part of my recovery was my faith. As an infant, I was baptized Catholic and raised by my family in the Catholic faith. I attended Mass on Sundays because that is what our family did, and I went along out of obligation. Even though going to Mass was something I had to do, I always enjoyed the gospel stories where Jesus would tend to the sick, the poor, and the outcasts. As I laid in bed while in the hospital when I was severely depressed, the Gospels came alive for me and became instrumental in my recovery over the months and years ahead.

The first gospel passage that came to mind was John 10:10, "A thief comes only to steal and slaughter and destroy; I came so that they might have life and have it more abundantly." I then reflected on my situation. I was in a crisis situation where I was paralyzed with fear. I could no longer care for myself and had gotten to where I wanted to die. I was certainly in a place where I *felt* destroyed. Not completely, but from where I was, the only thing separating me from total destruction was death.

Where I was, my confidence was destroyed, my happiness was destroyed, my hope was destroyed, my ambition was destroyed, my trust for others and in myself was destroyed, my sense of self-worth was destroyed, and so was my will to live. I certainly felt as though I was wallowing in destruction and began to think of the one who comes to destroy as the thoughts in my head were filling me with such negativity. Those thoughts I was having that I didn't matter, that I was worthless and unlovable.

It became apparent to me that I was certainly under the influence of the one who seeks to destroy. Once I realized this, I took it very personally. To have life, and to have it more abundantly, I would have to fight for it.

I began to consider how I had become victimized by the one who comes to destroy. I'm not talking about being possessed by demons, but how I had been influenced by destructive thoughts. I began to think of the one who seeks to destroy and He who came to give me life, and to have it more abundantly as two voices in my head. Much like the devil on one shoulder and an angel on the other whispering in my ear we think of when faced with a moral dilemma. Now I thought of the two fighting for my life within my thoughts. I was in control of my thoughts and it was now a matter of which one I would tune in to. Throughout my recovery, it would be an ongoing battle to sort through the lies and the deception of the one who seeks to destroy and an ongoing effort to connect with the One who brings life.

I also developed an awareness of how evil also has subtle ways of diminishing our lives by creating doubt in our minds, telling us we're not good enough and finding reasons why our great ideas won't work, thus killing our ambitions. It not only seeps into our minds by way of our negative thinking, it also finds its way through naysayers, and yes, even though those who may have our best interests at heart. It thrives on insecurity and seduces us to procrastinate and become distracted from our goals. It creates fear of failure that stops us from pursuing success. It takes swipes at our self-esteem and self-worth through illusions created in the media as news focuses on fear, and advertising preys on our insecurities. Through all this, it distorts the truth of who we are and what God has created us to be.

Self Doubt

Part of my recovery was going back to school and starting college. This gave me structure and a reason to get up and get on with my day. I had no idea what I would major in or what it would amount to, but I had in my mind I would get a bachelor's degree. At this time most of my friends were about to graduate from college because they started right after high school. I did not. Mostly because I hated high school and didn't want to. When I took a deeper look inside I also felt I wasn't smart enough to earn a bachelor's degree.

As I started I was scared. What if I fail? What if I can't actually hang in college? Then what would I do with my life? I shared my concerns about my lack of smartness with a counselor at the college. He gave me the best response to my uncertainty that I continue to use today anytime I have about with self-doubt. I told him I was afraid I might not be smart enough. He told me, "prove it." He went on to explain that in order for me to prove it I would need to do all the work, show up to class every day, study diligently and ask for help when needed from my teacher or a tutor. I had to put 100% effort into it. If I did that and at the end of the semester I was indeed failing... maybe we could say I wasn't smart enough. If that was the result, then he would have me tested for a learning disorder. I did the work as he prescribed and passed all my classes the first semester.

I no longer had any doubt of my ability to do college-level work as a result of "proving it." I still, however, had no idea what I would major in and couldn't imagine having a career of any kind, so I was taking random general education programs to try them out. I was at least earning credits that would transfer to a university, which was my ultimate goal, even though I didn't know exactly where that would be or what I would end up studying.

"I can do all things through Christ, who strengthens me." (Philippians 4:13) became my mantra anytime I felt the paralysis of self-doubt starting to consume me.

In my second semester, I took a speech class. On the first day of class, the professor told us public speaking was the number one fear of people in America. Fear was a big part of my debilitating depression. In my recovery, I was determined to eradicate fear from within myself. When I heard public speaking was people's worst fear, I then declared my major as Speech Communications. I figured if I could conquer public speaking, I could do anything.

I also began tackling fear in other ways. I was afraid to ask women out on dates. One of the many facets that led to my depression was growing up feeling insecure about my appearance. I was a skinny kid who got picked on because of it. Girls also made fun of how skinny I was. As I result I figured no woman would want to date me. So as part of my recovery, I decided to ask several women out for a date. I went even further and focused on women I deemed to be completely out of my league. I was terrified for my first approach, but then it got easier. I even scored a couple of dates. More importantly, none of them reacted negatively as I feared they would. The ones who declined did so graciously.

What I've learned about fear is the only way to get over a fear is to do the very thing you're most afraid of, so long as it doesn't endanger you. Ask yourself, "What's the worst thing that could happen?" Then ask if you can live with that. If it won't kill or harm you, push through the fear and go for what you want.

Today I'm an experienced professional speaker and I still get nervous before an appearance. I choose not to let my fear stop me. Fear is just another tool that evil uses to squash our motivation. I share my story of how God's grace healed me. I'm sure the devil would love for me not to.

"Be not afraid." (Mathew 17:7)

Love Never Fails

Ultimately what brought me to fully recovering from my depression was learning to love and accept myself completely. Getting there was a lot of work. This also came about through reflecting on the gospels. The greatest commandment of all Jesus tells us is, "Love the Lord your God with all your heart, and with all your soul and with all your mind, and with all your strength. This is the greatest and the first commandment. The second is like it, you must love your neighbor as yourself." (Mathew 22:37-39). The latter is just as important as the former. I figured I must love myself before I can fully love my neighbor. You can't give what you don't have. I can only give love to my neighbor as long as I have a love for myself.

The same is true if I am to love God with all my heart, mind and soul. It's a two-way street. How can I fully experience God's love for me if I feel I'm not good enough if I feel insecure and if I'm afraid? "Love has no room for fear" (1 John 4:18). "We were made in His image" (Genesis 1:27). "God is Love" (John 4: 8). Therefore, love is what we're made of. When we think less of ourselves we essentially tell God what He created is not good enough. When we fully love ourselves and embrace all that is love, we are free from fear and anxiety and create the life of abundance that Jesus said he came to give us.

What is Love?

1 Corinthians chapter 13:1-8 spells it out clearly for us.

Love is patient. When I am patient I am free of anxiety and aggravation. I am at peace.

Love is kind. When I am kind to others, it's a reflection of how I see myself because I was created out of love. I see my connection to others and I seek to serve others. I've learned serving others is a key ingredient to success.

Love rejoices with the truth. Truth is in understanding who we are, created as very good (Genesis 1:13) and in seeing that same value in others. The truth will set you free (John 8:32).

Love believes all things. Believing all things are possible through love. Belief is another essential ingredient to success. You must believe you will achieve.

Love hopes all things. Without hope, defeat can take hold. Obstacles and setbacks will occur along your way, but hope keeps your dream alive and gives you the energy to persevere.

Love never fails. There are only three guarantees in life that I am aware of. Our physical bodies will all die someday. God loves us (John 13: 34). The third is love never fails. When we love ourselves and others the same, we cannot fail. If we believe and hope all things, we cannot fail. When we live in the truth of who we are and are not derailed by fear and doubt, we cannot fail.

When I came to understand love in this way, my life completely changed from the despair I was in when I was depressed to creating a life filled with joy and success. I've succeeded in my education and now hold a Master's degree, which is something I once thought would never be possible. I married the love of my life, something I thought would never happen to me, and we have two beautiful, amazing children. I've run five full marathons, including two world majors and numerous half marathons, something I would never have anticipated. The setback of my depression propelled me to create the life I now experience.

In spite of my joyous life, setbacks have continued to be part of my life, but the lessons I learned through my recovery from depression -- along with my faith -- have given me the tools to propel me to reinvent myself and create new successes.

Creating My Purpose

My purpose has changed many times in my life. Coming out of depression my only purpose was to love and to do so meant fully loving and accepting myself. It meant being a good husband and father. It meant being of service to others. I really didn't think much of my purpose being part of my career. I just thought of my work as part of being a good husband and father. My work provided financial means to support my family.

I've had a variety of jobs throughout my life and my longest stretch of work was in law enforcement. Not because I ever really aspired to do so. It was a matter of me needing a job at the time and they were hiring. It provided a good income and good benefits and best of all I only had to do it four days a week. However, I didn't like being away from my family and working so much. I didn't like seeing the worst in people day in and day out. People only call the police when there is a problem and when they are in the midst of their worst nightmare. But I stuck with it because it was the responsible thing to do. I was able to provide for my family.

I began to feel that I wanted to do something other than police work and instead do something I would enjoy. I wanted to work as a counselor at a college or university.

When I looked into the requirements for admittance into the graduate program for this area of study, I encountered another setback. GPA requirement for an undergraduate degree was 3.0 to be eligible to apply for the program. I graduated with a 2.65 GPA so I was technically ineligible.

That technicality could have prevented me from even applying, but I was determined to still give it a shot. Because if I was, in fact, going to be denied, I wanted to at least do everything I could to make it happen. I contacted the head of the program and asked to meet with her to discuss my desire to be in the program. She agreed to meet with me. I put on my best suit to meet her at her office where I expressed my desire to do this. She was sold on my passion and agreed to accept me into the program under one condition. I had to be on academic probation for the first semester of the program. I had to take three classes and could do no worse than two As and one B. I finished the first semester with straight A's.

By the time I graduated and began looking for work at colleges and universities, I quickly realized that leaving my job with the police department and taking an entry-level position in this field would mean I would be taking a fifteen to twenty thousand dollar a year cut in pay. It didn't make any sense to me at the time. So I stayed.

As time went on I became more and more dissatisfied with my job. I really wanted to help people in a positive way. I never got my license to be a counselor, so that option was no longer on the table. I had talked to some friends who suggested I look into life coaching. I knew a friend from church who had become a life coach and consulted with him. In all, I liked what life coaching had to offer and felt it fit perfectly with what I wanted to do. I figured with only working four days a week I would be able to build a coaching practice with the other three days of the week and eventually be able to quit my job.

God had other plans. After thirteen years with the department, a declining economy led to a reduction in force, and I was laid off. I was stuck with... Now what? I wasn't given any severance pay and unemployment paid very little in comparison to what I was making. Building a business now would be a challenge with having no capital to invest in it. On the other hand, I did have time.

With my Master's degree, I was able to teach as an adjunct professor at the local community college where I got to teach a course called Educational, Career and Personal Development. I loved teaching this course. It really had an impact on students' lives. It was also an educational experience for me in learning what was going on in the minds of the students.

In the course, students are assigned guided journals to write in. In one of the journals, students are asked to write about their self-esteem and it's broken down into three parts. In the first section, students are asked to list ten of their best qualities. In the second section, students are asked to list ten of their weaknesses or areas they would like to improve upon. In the third section, students are asked to rate their level of self-esteem on a scale of one to ten.

What students wrote was quite revealing, particularly with what women wrote. On average on the scale from one to ten women ranked their self-esteem at 5.8. On average the men ranked theirs at 7.2. I also noticed many of the women fell short of making a list of best qualities and went beyond ten when listing their weaknesses. When listing their weaknesses most of the women were critical of their physical appearance in some way where the men rarely were.

This brought back memories of my experience counseling students during my internship as a graduate student working in the counseling center at the university. Out of all the students, I worked with there, only one of them was a male. All the female students I counseled had similar issues with lack of self-esteem and depression or anxiety.

I also considered how I had grown up in a family with only sisters and no brothers. In my teenage years, I was the guy who girls enjoyed talking to but never wanted to date because I was "too good as a friend." All of this collectively propelled me to what is now the primary focus of my coaching practice. I work with women to help them transform their lives into becoming fully empowered and self-confident.

What Drives You?

It became apparent to me how we live in a culture where women are bombarded with ads and commercials that are geared towards improving their outer appearance. There is everything from weight loss products and routines to products for better makeup and shinier hair to the latest fashion trends. All this appears to provide a way to improve your life, not to mention the $16 billion a year spent on plastic surgery in our country.

Yet with all this, it's estimated <u>1 in 4 women are taking some form of medication for depression and/or anxiety</u>. <u>$20 billion a year is spent in America on the weight loss industry</u> and <u>20 million women are suffering from some form of an eating disorder</u>. To me, it seems there is an underlying sense of low self-worth that contributes to these numbers.

I want to change this dynamic in our world. I want women to truly become fully empowered and self-confident. I want them to know and understand the truth of who they are and see it has nothing to do with their appearance. I want to see them eat healthy and exercise because it's a form of self-care and not because they're trying to fit into a size zero. Because when women, and also men, come to love themselves completely, they do great things and create great things. I'm a feminist, which means I believe men and women have equal value. Yes, we are different, and when we can see the value in our differences and work collaboratively to build each other up to be our best, we'll have it made.

The Kingdom of God is within you (Luke 17: 21).

Naysayers

Another passage I found helpful through my recovery from depression was John 14:6, "I am the way, and the truth and the life." Growing up I got a lot of negative messages from others through bullying from my peers and even some influential adults that contributed to my sense of low self-worth. I learned that it wasn't so much what others had said that was so destructive to me as it was that I believed what they said. If Jesus said, "I am the truth, the way and the life," I began to think that Jesus would never tell me the things that bullies and others had told me. Therefore, they can't be true, and I could instantly nullify them.

With the focus on my coaching practice working with women, I've had my share of naysayers. Mainly because I am a man and somehow to some being a man is a problem. I've been turned down from speaking at women's conferences because, well, they only wanted women to present. I've set up shop at women's events and was told once, "I would never discuss my self-esteem issues with a man." I once did a workshop at a women's boutique for women coming out of a divorce. A few days before the event a woman came into the boutique and spoke to the owner -- a woman. This woman asked the owner, "how could she have *a man* talk to women about getting through a divorce?" In my defense, the owner told the woman, "I guess we won't be expecting you."

My appeal when I encounter naysayers is, "who better?" With my education, training, and experience helping women to fully realize their potential and self-worth, along with my passion and desire to help them fully embrace who they are, it's not just what I do, it's my mission.

What Defines You?

The catalyst for me to openly share my story of overcoming depression came about through a coaching session I had with my peer coach during my coach training. We had to write our biography and it would be shared with the class. I wouldn't be who I am today without having gone through and recovered from depression. I knew this would be part of my story but was reluctant to make it known to the class.

My coach asked a great question, "How does having been depressed define you?"

I thought for a minute or two then responded, "It doesn't." She then asked, "So then what does?"

Without hesitation and with conviction I answered, "The fact that I kicked it's ass."

Whatever adversity you face or setback you encounter is an opportunity. Your greatest power in life is in the choices you make. You may not have control over your circumstance in life, but you get to choose how you respond to it. You are love. Be patient, be kind, believe, hope, and you will have the power to change your life, achieve your goals and live life abundantly.

***

Craig Nielson serves as a coach, motivational speaker, and advocate for women. He specializes in coaching women to become fully empowered by building stellar self-confidence and breaking down all barriers of insecurity and self-doubt. At the age of 21, he was hospitalized for three weeks for severe depression. From that very dark place in his life, Craig made a full recovery with professional help, exercise, and finding healing in the Gospels along with the love of God's grace. During a 13-year career in law enforcement, Craig worked with victims of sex crimes, domestic battery, and sexual assault. Wanting to work more proactively to help people, he returned to school to earn his Master's Degree in Counseling and Educational Psychology. With that, he went on to teach student success and personal development to college students. While counseling college students, Craig noticed a common thread with many female students suffering from low self-esteem and poor self-image. From there he knew his collective life experience had prepared him for his true calling: coaching women to become fully empowered and fearless. Craig continued his education and has received certification as a Professional Coach through iPEC (the Institute for Professional Excellence in Coaching) and is a Certified Christian Professional Coach through YKI (Your Kingdom Inheritance) Coaching. Today, Craig lives a positive and healthy lifestyle in Reno, Nevada with his wife of 24 years, daughter, and son. Craig is an avid runner and has completed 5 marathons, including the prestigious Boston and New York City marathons.

CANCELLED FLIGHTS AND CONNECTIONS

Jennifer Baker

This book is full of stories about overcoming setbacks as well as ways to overcome and propel yourself forward to make a difference in the lives of those who may be going through something similar. Some stories are miraculous, heart-breaking and others are tragic.

I am grateful to have been chosen to contribute to this book. Like the other authors, I too have had great trials in my life that I've had to overcome. From growing up in a broken home, surviving major surgeries and going to high school in a body cast as a teenager; to multiple financial setbacks, discovering my child had special needs as we nearly lost her, and ultimately almost losing my own life multiple times. I was honored to be asked to contribute to this book and excited to share some of my tools to launch forward and become a champion of situations.

However, this chapter is not about any of those stories. When I sat down to write, the story I was inspired to tell was not about overcoming my own tragedies. The message I wanted to share was how tragic it is that we live in a world with millions of people around us, yet we feel so disconnected from each other.

So often it seems people choose to let simple stresses grow into great frustration or adversity, rather than stopping to realize the beauty and lessons in whatever situation they are facing. We do this to ourselves and it causes us to further disconnect from those we are actually meant to be connected to. Tragedy is different for everyone. Simple annoyances in life can be made so large in someone's mind that they choose to ruin other people's days, lives, spirit, well-being and sadly sometimes even taking it as far as ending a life.

In all my travels, I hear stories of past business travelers or families who have their flights canceled or changed due to circumstances outside their control. I myself have been frustrated with cancellations that have left me stranded and struggling for alternative routes, and have witnessed enraged strangers who have many times been delayed alongside me. I've listened to their complaints about all the difficulties they've been put through, having to switch flights, sometimes even things as difficult as sleeping in the airport for days. I have even heard of incidents when people become so enraged that it has led to abuse, or sadly even getting thrown in jail.

I'm sure you can recall having a flight cancelled or delayed for yourself. When it happens to you it seems as though it is very personal and painful. There are over a half million average commercial flights *per day* in the United States. In an incredibly complex, but highly effective system, cancellations still happen all too often.

This chapter is about my own flight cancellation, which at the time I had no idea was going to be one of the most important flights I would ever miss. I believe what I learned from this experience is something all "life travelers" need to know.

I woke up mentally and physically exhausted from a multi-day campaign tour and back-to-back meetings travelling, learning, and strategizing with a new friend whom I had just agreed to work with on their campaign

I already felt like the day had been incredibly special. 'The Judge" and I were both excited to go home, he to his best friend and wife of 40+ years, and me to my family who were anxiously awaiting my arrival. I enjoy mostly working from home, and though I video chat with my two kids all the time when I travel, I still miss them like crazy. There is nothing like the welcome home celebration of my animals and teenagers. We have a private homecoming ritual that is strong enough to make any bad day melt away instantly. I really needed that tonight as the stress of some very heavy life issues were weighing on me, mixed with this exhaustion.

Our last meeting of this week's trip still had my head swimming in thoughts of how blessed I felt to have experienced all that I had that day. I had been praying and meditating on what my role was to be and if I was doing the right thing for about a week. After my lessons from this adventure I knew I was exactly where I was supposed to be.

Our host graciously gave us a back-of-the-house tour after my starry-eyed request. I wish I could explain it; something rocked my energy as we entered the building and waited for our meeting to begin. From the parking lot I recognized that something incredible was about to happen during this meeting, but I never imagined what I'd see inside.

Hours later my body was still feeling positive vibrations from the energy in the meeting. The photos, plants, colors, textures and paintings throughout the huge building had all added to those feelings for me. The individual offices clearly defined each person's beliefs and personality with unique styles. Their personal office environment was created uniquely for/by them to be a motivational respite for each individual, yet every office also had a common theme that fit the energy of the entire building. This created one of the most beautiful working environments I've ever witnessed. I wondered if this was the new generation of business practices that I had envisioned and had been trying to create for my clients; one that supports the uniqueness of the individual while encouraging working together as a whole.

Years ago I had opened a consulting firm and had strived to create a new generation of business that aligned others with the same core values and business practices, while uniting co-workers, community, families and government.

Over a decade ago I made the decision to **only** engage in business practices with those that were working to make a difference. I found and created ways to show businesses how to contribute what each individual and organization knew they were called to contribute. I was very proud to be a person whose business was built as both 'heart core' and hard core about making a real difference in the world.

While walking through this beautiful business complex, the cynical side kept asking if this was real or a façade. My optimistic side was so excited that I had a hard time staying composed and focused on the reason for our meeting until we sat down in their board room where I let go and unconsciously 'gave it to God.'

The room had some of the most incredible spiritual artwork I had ever seen. Every seat at this huge, old-world wooden table with its chairs reminded me of tables in religious pictures resembling the last supper. The walls were lined with Catholic pews and the ceiling looked like a Cathedral.

Let me be clear, I'm not Catholic, but I respect that we all have religious/spiritual beliefs, and over the years I have enjoyed spending time with people of all kinds. This day I was completely moved by the way this room made me feel closer to God and full of purpose. That feeling still calls my heart and mind back to those moments even months after the visit. And they continued with me as we departed to make our flight home.

The Judge and I made it to the airport with double the time to spare, so we decided on eating at the healthiest restaurant we could find. As we ate at the 'community table' with other strangers, we enjoyed the conversation and kept things very light hearted to help us change gears before we went back to our home life.

Grabbing my phone, I double checked the gate numbers for our flight and discovered that our flight was delayed. Soon after that it was cancelled. I was perplexed because we don't usually see cancellations like this, as it was less than a 90-minute flight to our home.

I called the airline and started trying to figure out the best options for a different route home. I asked if the Judge had preferences. His simple answer was firm and clear: "I don't care how we get there, I just want to get home tonight."

We made our way over to what was supposed to be our gate. Lining up behind several other irate travelers, we could overhear their concerns. I was on the phone with the reservations agent trying to figure out why the flight was cancelled and wasn't getting any clear reason. All they would say were the flights were cancelled and offered to re-route us to many locations, but none would get us home that night.

The best they could do was get us in sometime the next day. This was not an option for the judge, or for me, so I became a little more creative and started making suggestions to help them think outside the box. I'd done this before and I was prepared to do it again tonight. I told the attendants to book our flights. We would make it home even if I had to drive us over the mountains in the wind and snow.

One of the beautiful attendants assisting the other line of stranded and frantic guests overheard my statement and stopped to look over at me with a puzzled look. She said the weather was the factor, so she wasn't sure that would work. I told her, "I have two beautiful children waiting for me at home so this will work out just fine, with a little grace, trust, and cooperation." The attendant giggled and said, "I'll do my part," and worked on making that happen.

The Judge stepped away to call his wife and tell her the news. As the frazzled attendants were taking care of the details, I spun around to all the other stranded passengers who were complaining about the lack of service and ability to help them. They would not accept that the flights were cancelled. They were frustrated and unwilling to accept defeat.

The woman behind me was now discussing with the attendant her options after listening in and kept staring at me for answers. There was another man three people behind me who had a very concerned look on his face but just kept quiet. I heard him say to himself, "I have to get home, I have no other option because I have court at 8 o'clock."

I felt most drawn to this troubled man, but he was so far back that I hadn't had the chance to talk to him or find out his story. The look on his face concerned me most. I don't know what hit me, I just opened my mouth and out it came. I looked directly into this man's eyes and at the people directly behind me and said, "Join us, we'll be creative and play planes, trains, and automobiles if we have to. I WILL get us home tonight, no matter what."

The man with the very concerned look on his face stepped out of line and walked over to me. He was tall with a strong athletic build. Even in my 4-inch heels he towered over me, yet I could sense his kind spirit. He introduced himself as Molech, and asked me why I invited him to join us. After some discussion back-and-forth about our plan, Molech shared that he wasn't sure I was serious and didn't know what to think. "Most people don't do this, invite perfect strangers to join them." However, he explained he had court in the morning to deal with a very sensitive case regarding children and couldn't miss it, or he would be postponing some critical issues around their well-being.

I certainly hadn't planned on announcing to complete strangers that they should join me on a road trip, but also didn't understand why he or the others would question my invitation. I only knew that they needed to get home as much as the judge and I did. There was no doubt I was going home, so if they needed to get there as much as we did, they should be with us so I could help them and make sure they were safe.

Others began weighing the idea and their trust in the situation, no doubt. Two people chose other routes, and several chose to remain in LA until the next day, but two of the men agreed to make the trip. One even offered to take care of the rental car. Two of our passengers needed to get their luggage from baggage claim downstairs and needed to come all the way back through check-in and TSA in order to get on the next flight to start our new route. The men quickly let go of the irritation and stress surrounding the urgent need to get home and accepted the new route as a suitable creative option.

Before they left on their baggage claim journey, Molech stepped away to make a call and another traveler, Tom, and I briefly talked about our options. He let me know that both he and his wife were retired police officers, so I could trust him travelling with us. He mentioned going to a fundraiser to meet my friend and U.S. Senator who had started mentoring my son, as well as a very prominent attorney in town that was one of my good friends. We took a selfie together and sent it to this friend just for fun and to see his reaction. We laughed and shared our ideas of his reaction when he received the playful but unexpected text.

Molech chose to stay with me as the other two started on their baggage journey. Without realizing it we started into a very deep conversation, which led us to realize our hearts were aligned long before we met. We had a mutual protective interest in a certain family, a group of people, had several friends in common, and the greatest part... we engaged in an incredible conversation and instantly knew we would be life-long friends. Molech and I realized this cancellation was meant to be, and our conversations took on the connectedness of two people doing their best to make a difference in the world through guidance and enlightenment.

By the time the other two returned from their baggage claim and TSA excursion, we were told to move to a new gate. We gathered all of our belongings and headed down a long hallway to a very secluded Gate 9. There was a lady sitting in front of us at a table for four, so I walked over and asked her if those seats were taken. She cautiously but graciously offered us seats. I introduced myself and asked her if she was also waiting for our flight.

The lady said her name was 'Linda' and she lived in a small town called Nevada City. I have a special affinity for her community and we all shared mutual friends, acquaintances, and stories of the city. She asked about each of us and we shared our stories and found many connection points to follow up on, especially the Judge. She said she didn't like politics but believed the world needed people like him to make a difference and wanted to support his campaign efforts.

Sitting to my left was another table and another professionally dressed man who was talking business on the phone while staring at his computer. He seemed very intense so I turned my back to focus on the group in front of me. Tom found a new friend off to the side against the wall and we occasionally watched them in their long-winded conversations. The Judge, Molech and I chose to stay and converse with Linda.

After about 45 minutes we were told the gate was closing. Without an explanation, we had to move back to our original gate number. We decided to stay in the room we were in because it was so quiet and we still had another hour to wait until our flight was to leave. We joked back-and-forth with the desk attendant but she was less than interested in our chatter.

Then Darius, the businessman off to my left, hung up the phone after concluding his intense conversation. I introduced everyone as though we were all long lost friends and we listened to his story about how he needed to be in the same city as us for a very big meeting in the morning with his team.

Something compelled me to ask what type of business he was in and he shared with me that the business was a unique I.T. start-up company. He was also a speaker who helped people understand that we are all one from the beginning and has scientific proof in his program that helps prove this is true.

After speaking to Darius and thinking about my day and all the connections I had made up to this point, I began to get teary-eyed. His logic was not only believable, but was also playing out right in front of me. He then went on to tell me who he had just recently been invited to speak for. We realized that we had mutual adoration for Houston and concern for the community. I had also just spoken there a few months before, doing similar work, trying to unite communities.

As Molech and I were listening to Darius talk we were both moved by all that was transpiring. My thoughts rolled back to earlier that evening when we had a very similar conversation while left alone at the gate. It started with Molech questioning me because he was baffled that a white, blonde-haired female so randomly offered to jump in the car for hours with a complete stranger—a black man who was raised street-wise, in a hard core area of California. He was perplexed that I didn't seem to have any thought of danger when I had invited him.

My response, "When I looked at you I didn't see color, or any danger issues, all I could see was a man with a beautiful energy, a kind heart and deep need to get home, so I didn't care whether we knew each other enough, or where you came from. I trust that God connected us through a need and that we could work together to get home to our community safely." He said, "Lady YOU are a rare person." My response, "That is too bad."

Darius pulled my attention back into his words with a simple but powerful statement, "We all need to realize how closely connected genetically we are and how we can prove it."

After Molech and I talked with Darius for a while we shared our other travel options and that he was welcome to ride with us if he wished. He considered it and after careful deliberation, called his wife and told her he was coming home to curl up where he belonged for the night. His team could handle the meeting in person and he would take it by video conference. Though he turned down our invitation, he enjoyed our conversation so much that he actually stuck around to talk to us for over an hour, waiting until our flight departed.

Before he left this newfound 'friend group,' we decided that we needed photos to solidify this moment and all of our connectedness. Just before we took the picture,

Sasha, our beautiful flight attendant who was working at the counter, came walking up the aisle.

Sasha's forced smile was magnetic before, but when she saw all of us together enjoying each other's company, she burst into laughter and yelled, "No way! What did I miss and what are you guys doing all the way over here?" We made her jump in the photos and told her we would explain the circumstances later. I sent a quick note of explanation after the trip because I felt she needed to know how instrumental she was in creating that special moment by trusting me and rerouting us.

We *finally* boarded the long-awaited plane over 3 hours after our direct 1+ hour flight was cancelled. The Judge and I sat together on the left side of the plane and the two other gentlemen sat one row in front and across the aisle from us. They talked briefly, then Molech quickly fell asleep.

The Judge tried to stay awake but quickly accepted sleep as the best option to avoid being exhausted the next day. I tried to sleep but the events of the day and my conversations, mostly with Molech and Darius still moved me, and my brain just kept reviewing the conversations.

We landed safely but not without weather and turbulence to shake us up a little first. We quickly launched into our next series of fun challenges to get our luggage, rental car and get on the road. Tom decided to drive and I sat in the backseat with Molech.

We continued our deep conversations on ways to change laws and the surroundings of those most vulnerable by leveraging our sphere of influence, knowledge and beliefs. We also shared some personal laughter at the situation and the incredible work performed that night for us to meet. Meanwhile, Tom was driving very slow and still telling stories of his own. As we all parted ways we agreed that our meeting and our connections were all meant to be.

After safely returning home many hours later and early in the morning. I had been up for over 26 hours, but I still couldn't turn off my mind from all of the amazing lessons I felt I had just learned. As I lay in my own bed, I continued quietly counting my blessings and asking, what do I do with what I have learned? So many answers came to me but the one most powerful was that I needed to share this story and its overall messages with as many people as I could.

I often glean meaning out of every situation I am in and my mind raced with so MANY lessons for days after this trip. Here are a few I felt compelled to share with you in the form of Jenn-ism's. My hope is to enlighten you that obstacles -- no matter how difficult -- are meant to be overcome. They are to teach us and give us something that we need, even if it's not something we always want.

1. Everything you do is a reflection of you. Maintain your character when facing any hardship or

challenge. In order to do this, you'll need to prioritize what's most important and hold tightly to it when you want to lash out. Often times we think our own issue is what's most important and that nothing else matters. That makes for precarious moments and sometimes we mistreat those around us who truly don't deserve it. Remember that the most important thing is to maintain your character and always treat those around you with kindness. Period.

2. ***Never*** accept failure as an option. There are always multiple answers to any challenge. Take the issue from a 30-60,000 foot view first, and if that doesn't help, take it further. You will see a solution and that will allow you to let go of the frustration. Humans often have an 'amygdala override' in stressful situations. You need to avoid this in order to think clearly and create a win-win for everyone around you.

3. Never let fear or ignorant superficial issues get in the way of doing what's right. No matter what issues may be in the way. Meeting Molech was an amazing opportunity for me. He told me it was life-changing for him. He was completely blown away that I wasn't in the least bit concerned about the color of his skin, or the fact that he was a male, with a very strong

physical build. I didn't even notice other than to have a basic physical description (nor should anyone else).

I did what I felt compelled to and asked him to come with. I would do it 1,000 times over if given the chance again. For those who feel this world is full of racism, I don't agree. I'm not saying that doesn't exist. I just call it individual and group ignorance, and damaged people who damage others to make themselves feel better.

The same people who are calling names or making cruel statements -- regardless of sex, race, creed, sexual preferences, etc. -- are usually the same ones who call their brothers, sisters, neighbors, friends and everyone else around them bad names. They are people who like to hurt others and are weak so they need to be prayed for and educated. But I never give them strength in what they do by giving them a title they may be proud of, or use to make others feel weak.

Every one of us brings something unique and amazing to the world and just because we may look or act different we are still all connected. Together we can co-create a magnificent world to live in for each of us. Separate we can destroy everything around us, including our beautiful world, which if left unbiased and without prejudice is full of love, care, and the most incredible opportunities for success that humans have ever experienced.

4. Always be open to the messages from our Creator. Every situation, no matter how frustrating or painful it is, is an **opportunity**. Whether it's learning, growing, tolerating or just simply taking the 30,000-foot view to see and seize your opportunity, allow it to mold you into a better person, leveraging the lesson you found in your opportunity.

5. There are no mistakes or accidental meetings. Every person who affects or enters your life is there for a reason, a season or a lifetime. Acknowledge, appreciate and respect who they are to you, always. We are all connected in some way. If they're in your space, there is something to glean from their presence.

The number one thing that I learned from this cancelled flight and the next few cancelled flights that followed, is when our life isn't going as planned and we are stopped in our tracks, we need to look around at our fellow passengers, and reach out our hands. God has halted you in place for a reason and if you are just open to reaching out to those around you, then you will be amazed at how cancelled plans can actually make for the very best connections.

***

A powerful force to work with, Jennifer Baker is an Internationally recognized Business and Motivational Speaker, Executive Coach, a Master Certified Expert for Digital Marketing, business and political consultant and the creator of the Success GPS Programs and Seminars. Jennifer was invited to co-author an overnight Best-Seller, 'The Road to Success" Volume 2 with Jack Canfield in 2016 and Launch in 2017. Jennifer has been selected as one of America's Premier Experts™, and internationally recognized as one of the Top 100 Most Influential people from Influence Magazine. Jennifer spends her time speaking to, training, and supporting tens of thousands of companies that range from start-up companies and 'Dream-preneurs' to Fortune 100 companies worldwide, and has multiple awards from the most important people in her life as Best Mom in the World. She 'retired' in her 30's from her executive-level position to pursue her purpose of helping others create a positive life of balance and impact. Jennifer shows her clients how to increase success through ethics, values and socially conscious efforts and business development so they have enough money to live the life they want and still be able to be a good parent or mentor for the next generation. Jennifer is passionate about helping businesses and executives create a positive ripple effect in business and professional climates, which is the best support for our nation's economic and family stability.

TRUST AND LET GO

Sylvia J. Harral, M. Ed., N.C.

Like a pebble in a slingshot, my passion for helping people take charge of their health lay pinched between 1) my knowledge of what to do, and 2) a lack of confidence in my ability to meet people's needs. My greatest goal was to have a business that instilled two things in people. 1) The knowledge of what a truly healthy body is like, and 2) The desire and ability to live in one. Try as I might to reach my goals, I felt the "Y-Stick" of ideas and decisions moving in that direction, but lack of knowledge and confidence stopped my business from flowing the way that I wanted it to.

I attended seminar after seminar, took classes, read books, talked to family, friends, and coworkers, made lists of goals and objectives, tried to write business plans, and "What I Do" statements. I wrote "To Do" lists and "Wish" lists, elevator speeches and Powerpoint presentations.

In the midst of all this busyness, I saw my decisions and ideas moving forward, but my business growth stayed frozen. My passion was like that pebble being pinched between these two strong mindsets, and the last thing that I felt I was able to do was to let go. The struggle within continued until fate took over and drove my car into a guardrail and tree at 60 miles per hour.

Suddenly everything changed!

It was in the fall of 2015. I was feeling pretty successful teaching my college health course that had taken over 15 years to design and perfect. Then an upper respiratory issue started going around, and the symptoms didn't skip over me like I thought they should. I caught a cold and was not happy with my immune system for allowing my body to get sick.

My business was a little herbal pharmacy and health education service. There were several things in the store that would boost my immune system, but I decided to try a new product called ImunStem and its companion product, Aktiffvate. They were from a local Nutraceutical company whose products weren't even on the market yet.

When I went to the company to pick up the products, the scientist who made them met me. He said, "If you ever cut yourself or have surgery, your body won't bleed as much. The ImunStem will strengthen your blood vessels." I certainly had no intention of cutting myself or having surgery of any kind. But I listened, nodded, thanked him and took the products every day for about three weeks. By then, the cold was long gone, and I started forgetting to take the supplements.

A few weeks after that, I was driving to town from my home in the foothills of the Sierra Nevada mountains. My dance team was scheduled to perform at a special person's

107th birthday party. It was around noon on Sunday, November 22, 2015. I was driving past the golf course when I felt a little bit sleepy. It was nothing unusual except for the gut feeling that said, "Stop the car. Pull over and wake yourself up!"

My thoughts immediately chimed in with, "It's noon, and you slept well last night. You just hauled two loads of wood and got plenty of exercise. Plus, you're going to be dancing soon. That keeps you awake."

My foot listened to my head instead of my gut and stayed on the gas pedal.

The next thing I knew, a man was asking me if I could move. I opened my eyes just enough to see that I was in my car, but it was stopped. The airbag was blown and lying across my lap and console. I tried to move my arms and legs, but nothing would move. I tried to answer the man by saying, "I can't move. Nothing moves." Even my lips wouldn't move.

I looked down at the airbag again and noticed a tiny movement. My blood was dripping onto the airbag. I realized what had happened and said to myself, "Oh, boy! I've really done it this time," and closed my eyes again.

There was no pain at that time, so my mind flashed back to something I had learned at one of the seminars. Dr. Sue Morter was telling us that everything happens to help us learn lessons. "We come into this life to learn," she said, and

242

she gave us three rules about learned lessons: 1. "The lesson will be learned." Then she added, "Many lessons are learned with the last breath." At the time she said that I remember making a decision to focus on learning my lessons. It would be better to spend the precious moments of my life basking in learned lessons rather than putting off the learning and going through a big cram session before the final exam. 2. "The lesson will be repeated until it's learned," and 3. "Each repeat gets harder."

"Oh, boy," I thought. "This lesson can't get much harder. I'd better learn it right now. But, what is the lesson?" I couldn't think of what it could be, and there was nothing I could do, so I drifted back to sleep.

Although many parts of my body were injured and broken, there was no pain. I was in total shock and alone with one thought, "What is the lesson I need to learn?"

The next thing I knew, a man was giving a command, "Hold her head. Don't let it move. Whatever we do, don't let that head move!"

I felt strong hands press against both sides of my neck and head. I knew I was being taken out of the car, but I felt nothing except the strong hands. My total focus was on the secure feeling those hands gave me. I was okay in those hands. They stayed pressed against my neck for what seemed like a long time. There was nothing I could do but be totally submissive to whatever was happening to me.

The next thing I knew, a pair of scissors was sliding up my right leg cutting away my jeans. "Well," I thought, "there goes that pair of pants. Hmm, which pair of pants am I wearing?" I wondered about it, but there was nothing I could do, so I drifted back to sleep in total submission.

Then I heard the faint sound of a helicopter in the distance. It grew louder and I realized that I was going to be taking a ride inside that big bird. "Oh, boy," I said to myself. "That's going to be a pretty penny." I began to wonder how all of these people were going to get paid. How much was it going to cost me? How in the world would I ever pay for this? What is the lesson I'm supposed to learn?

As the helicopter lifted off, I wondered where they were taking me. The hospital in town wasn't far away, and in a few moments, I knew we had flown right over town. They were taking me somewhere else. I couldn't imagine where, and there was nothing I could do but go along for the ride.

I don't recall the helicopter ride ending or all the busyness of 13 hours in the emergency room. There is a faint recollection of them straightening my broken left ankle. My body jerked, and someone said, "Oh, she felt that."

The most vivid recollection of those hours was when I found myself looking at a large red circle. I imagined I was looking at the big spot of blood that had dripped on the blown airbag. I wasn't sure if it was that particular spot of blood, but it didn't matter. The spot was slowly shrinking in size from a large platter to a small saucer.

Then it stopped. Everything was still. It was suffocatingly still. My lungs and heart had even stopped. I thought, "Is this what it's like to die? Well, this won't take long." In all my lifesaving, nursing, and CPR training, I had learned that four minutes is all the brain can survive without oxygen. There was nothing I could do but submit ... to the ultimate. There was no fear ... no pain ... no struggle ... just drifting back to sleep.

Back in town, one of my dancers telephoned Golden Sunrise Nutraceutical, the maker of ImunStem and Aktiffvate. She said to the scientist, "Sylvia has been in a bad car accident and is in the hospital in Fresno. Do something!"

"Okay," he said.

"Please," she begged. "Do something for her. She needs you right now."

"Okay," he said again, "I got it."

"Please," she continued. "You're the only one that knows what to do and she needs you ..."

"Okay," he interrupted. "I'm in the lab right now, and I need to hang up so I can go do something."

"Oh! Okay, thank you."

He worked in the lab that night gathering a special combination of herbs and putting them through the technology that is so unique to the product line from Golden

Sunrise Nutraceutical. The next morning, he and another staff member drove to Fresno Community Hospital Trauma Center with the little bottle of precious herbs. He found me in the Trauma Center with a breathing machine in my throat. IVs, catheters and casts were everywhere. He was faced with a real dilemma. How was he going to get these special herbs into my body? That was unthinkably impossible in that situation without the total coincidence that revealed itself right then.

My niece was a traveling nurse. Two months prior to my accident, she had taken her next three-month assignment as a Trauma nurse at Fresno Community Hospital Trauma Center. Coincidently, she and I were now on the same floor. She wore all the badges and had all the training on all the machines I was hooked up to. In a few seconds, she had the herbal formula in my body.

One of the machines was checking my blood pressure automatically every 15 minutes. The pressure was running at 135/40. Five minutes after receiving the herbs, my diastolic pressure climbed to 55. That was significant. Even though the diastolic returned to 40 a little while later, the herbs had made their impact.

As the hours and days progressed, I became more and more awake. The lesson I was to learn came clear. It had been there from the last moment before hitting the guardrail and tree. "LISTEN TO YOUR GUT!" I knew that, but I wasn't practicing it very well. It's great to know something but knowing is nothing compared to acting on it.

There is a thing in our body called the Gut-Brain Connection. The gut is actually "The Second Brain." We all know what it's like to get that gut feeling about something. When we follow our gut, we are never sorry. There is a scripture that says, "The spirit of man is the candle of the Lord; searching all the inward parts of the belly." The ability to listen to that still, small voice of guidance is something we must develop through trial and error. Some people call it God's voice that speaks through the gut. The reason it is still and small is because God speaks with only one voice ... silence. That's why it's so hard to hear Him. One must listen very, very carefully to pick up what He's saying. When the mouth is busy translating all the neuron-firing activity in the brain, it's impossible for the ears to pick up the messages that are trying to come through from the gut. The messages that lead to greatness are coming through the silence. Submission opens the ears to a more keen discernment of the language of guidance.

Listening to my gut was the first lesson I was to learn from my major setback. As I recovered from the shock, I realized how weak my whole body was. My muscles didn't have enough strength to move anything. I remembered a scripture that said, "They that wait on the Lord shall renew their strength. They shall mount up with wings like eagles.

They shall run and not be weary; they shall walk and not faint." Those words had been set to music, and the song was playing in my head. As the song played, I felt invited to renew my strength by waiting on the Lord.

"Well, okay," I thought. "I'm waiting. I have nothing else to do but lie here and wait for the Lord to renew my strength." As I lay there, that thought began to seem ridiculous. Muscles don't gain strength by doing nothing. The way to build strength while you wait is to 'wait' like a waitress. The waitress waits on you by asking what you would like her to do for you or bring you. If I was going to "wait on the Lord," I needed to wait on Him like a waitress and ask Him what he wanted; then do what He told me.

When I asked what He wanted, I remembered the scripture that says, "I would that you prosper and be in health even as your soul prospers."

"That would make sense," I thought as the invitation became specific to take charge of my health right then and there; in the hospital. A healthy body can do more waitressing than an unhealthy one, so I began to move the muscles I could while respecting the parts that were broken.

As my body healed, I was moved to different parts of the hospital. They said they were "moving me closer to the door." I went from Trauma ICU, to Step-Down ICU, to the cardiac unit for a day, then to Rehab. In Rehab, I learned to sit on the edge of my bed, transfer to a wheelchair, stand up on one leg, and raise one knee to my chest. My strength was coming back ever so slowly as I waitressed my health.

Some of my dancers came to visit and they handed me an inspirational "Get Well" card. It had a picture of Christ carrying a person on the beach and making only one set of "Footprints in the Sand." I instantly saw myself in that picture and understood why I was still here. The moment my foot had decided to stay on the gas pedal, Christ scooped me up in His arms and carried me through those close calls and traumatic circumstances. I thought about all the things He obviously had His hand in and decided to coin a new name for Him: the "Choreographer-of-Coincidences". The safety I had felt in the hands that held my head and neck was fleeting compared to the trust I now felt in the arms of my Choreographer-of-Coincidences. I realized that everything in my life was already worked out. All I had to do was submit to Him and trust His guidance.

After that, I woke up with this song in my head:

"Out in the highways and byways of life, many are weary and sad.

Carry the sunshine where darkness is rife, making the sorrowing glad.

... Make me a blessing to someone today."

The invitation came to be a blessing to someone. "But who?" I thought. "How can I be a blessing in this hospital bed? I don't go anywhere or see anyone except nurses and a few visitors." Then the invitation focused on the request to "Bless My Nurses."

"Hmm," I thought. "Am I being asked to waitress my nurses? They're supposed to be taking care of me. I can't even get out of bed. How can I possibly bless them?"

I thought about my nurses. I got a new one every day. They walk in and introduce themselves to me and write their name on the message-board on the wall. They're tired, stressed, not happy sometimes as they focus on their procedures. They may even be wishing they were somewhere else. They don't know me. I'm just a body in this bed with an ugly tube sticking out my nose. They do a good job of making sure I'm getting everything my doctors ordered. And, they make sure I'm not doing anything I'm not supposed to do; like drinking water, because I might choke on it. My nurses are the ones I have the most contact with, so I began to practice my new "waitressing" skills on them.

When I greeted them, called them by name, thanked them for what they did for me, complimented them and was compliant and agreeable, they seemed to leave my room in a little better mood. This quickly became my new mission; to lie there in bed and "Bless My Nurses," while continuing to take charge of my health, of course. Life was starting to get busy.

Being agreeable and compliant with my nurses and doctors while taking charge of my health was an interesting challenge. Even though an IV was dripping fluid into my bloodstream, I could tell that my body was becoming more dehydrated. I shared my symptoms with my doctor and he changed the pain medication from Norco to Ibuprofen. The Ibuprofen needed to be crushed and mixed with water. It was given to me through my feeding tube, then the tube was rinsed with water. The process put a half cup of water in my body. Two pain medications a day gave me a total of one cup of water per day: not enough, but a start.

Up until then I had refused pain medication for two reasons, 1) Norco is an addictive narcotic, and 2) I was still feeling no pain. When the doctor allowed me to have more water by changing my medication, I began asking for it as often as I could.

Another example of taking charge of my health while blessing my nurses with compliance and agreement centered on the side effects of having that feeding tube.

My jaw had been broken in five places, so my mouth was wired shut. The only way to get food in my stomach was through a feeding tube. Since the tube went through the opening to the stomach, it was possible for the stomach acid to sneak along the side of the tube, through the opening, and up into the esophagus. This creates heartburn.

My nurse walked in and said, "I'm going to give you Protonix for heartburn."

"But I'm not having any heartburn," I said.

The nurse used her knowledge of body function to reason with me. She explained, "The doctors order it routinely for tube-feeding patients. The tube goes through the valve that normally closes and keeps the food in the stomach. Now the food can come back through the valve, up the esophagus and cause heartburn. All our tube-feeding patients take it." She started preparing it for me.

I thought for a second, then said, "Protonix stops hydrochloric acid by neutralizing it, right?"

"Yes," she said. "That's what burns the esophagus, and that's why we stop it."

"I certainly don't want heartburn," I said, "but doesn't hydrochloric acid digest protein as well?"

"Yes, it does," she answered as she continued preparing the Protonix.

"My body needs protein to make new bone and heal," I reasoned carefully, "so I need my hydrochloric acid to digest the protein that's coming in through my feeding tube, right?"

"Yes," she answered.

"And the head of my bed is elevated at 30° to prevent the stomach contents from going back up the esophagus, right?" I continued.

"Yes," she said.

"So, would it be okay to see if the 30° elevation is enough to take care of the heartburn? And if I start getting heartburn, I will call you for the Protonix immediately."

She stopped preparing the Protonix and didn't "cha-ching" my ankle bracelet for it either. I never had to call. Protonix was unnecessary for me. It felt good to refuse an unnecessary medication while being agreeable and compliant.

Having the Golden Sunrise Nutraceutical products in my body along with diligence at taking charge of my health helped shorten my stay in the hospital. After five weeks they sent me home.

On the way, I asked, "What will I do now that I have no more nurses to bless?" I thought about my little business. Then I remembered the way my nurses had brightened up with agreeable compliance from me. They weren't the only people who felt stressed and tired. Everyone in my community knows how that feels. The answer to my question was very clear. The invitation came to "Bless My Community."

It took a few months for my body to heal and strengthen enough to walk. Friends came to visit. One friend in particular, was the scientist from Golden Sunrise Nutraceutical. He brought another all-herbal supplement from his lab. This one helped my skin heal from the injuries, breaks, and needles. I was happy with the way this cream made my skin look and feel.

One by one the cast, external fixator, braces, and wires were removed. I began to think about a project my business partner and I had begun a few weeks prior to the accident. We had decided to write a column in the local newspaper. This way, people in our community could learn about how their body functions at the cellular level and be empowered to take charge of their health. We answered questions, gave healthy recipes and named the column "Tid-Bits of Health."

As the power of the Golden Sunrise Nutraceutical herbs assisted my recuperation, I began to write about the herbs in my articles. I wanted my readers to know that something amazing is coming from our town. The scientist would share information with me, and I would pass it on to my readers. One of the things he informed me about was the signing of a new law called "Twenty-First Century Cures Act."

Almost a year after I left the hospital, the President of the United States passed this new law. The law had nothing to do with me, but everything to do with the effectiveness of the all-herbal products from Golden Sunrise Nutraceutical. These formulas, which had done so much for me, had already made their way to the FDA, congressmen, and senators. The healing qualities of the herbs were impressing the leaders of this country.

The leaders looked at the research projects that were being conducted to find cures for diseases. They looked at the funding our government was pouring into those projects. Then they looked at the number of drugs and medications that were actually "curing" anything. Knowing that the body's immune system is the only thing that can "cure," they compared the results they were experiencing from ImunStem and Aktiffvate to the results they felt from other medications. They saw how these two products alone did more for building a person's immune system than any other medication or supplement.

They spent three years researching and writing the Twenty-First Century Cures Act, and on December 13, 2016, President Obama signed it. His signature earmarked a forthcoming shift in the way medicine would be practiced. On the day the Cures Act was signed, the scientist said to me, "Get going, Sylvia. Start treating people in the community with ImunStem and Aktiffvate."

While thinking long and hard about what to do, I saw two roadblocks. One was the taste of the products, and the other was the price. Both were a stretch.

Then one day a homeless man came in and said he had been diagnosed with brain cancer. "Give him a dose of ImunStem and Aktiffvate," my gut said. Before giving him the products, I asked about his pain level. On a scale of 1-10, his pain was an eight. I instructed him to hold the liquid under his tongue for two minutes, then drink a glass of water. Keeping it off the taste buds while the saliva reduced the strong flavor solved the taste problem. Ten minutes after taking the two products, his headache pain dropped down to a six. "If you come back tomorrow," I told him, "I'll give you another dose." He came back, and after his second dose, his pain level was a four.

I was concerned about giving away doses of these precious, rare supplements. Kings, presidents, and celebrities travel from around the world to get them. They pay thousands of dollars, and I'm giving it away to a homeless man. But, from my gut, I invited him to come back the third day.

He told me how amazing these products were, that he definitely felt a difference and liked how he felt. I asked if he had seen a doctor and received a diagnosis of brain cancer. He said he had, so I asked if he could bring me a copy of his lab results with the diagnosis. The medical team at Golden Sunrise Nutraceutical would review it when I told them what I was doing for him. He said he would bring it to me, but I never saw him again.

I went to the medical team without the paperwork and confessed that I had given doses of ImunStem and Aktiffvate to a homeless man. I felt a little concerned that the scientist might be upset that no money was coming in for all the knowledge and hard work that went into making the products. The scientist didn't hesitate to give me his answer. "Sylvia," he said, and gave the kind of pause that adds emphasis to his words, "we have to help our community."

Those words hit me like a great invitation to take the most unique, health-building products on the planet and "Bless my Community." Joy and confidence were released inside me. Those feelings grew over the next few days until a plan formed in my head.

The plan was a program that introduced people to ImunStem and Aktiffvate. They would receive doses of each product for 10 days. They would learn how to take it, and I would keep track of the results they experienced each day. When the 10 days were finished, they could decide to either 1) walk away, 2) sign up for another 10 days, or 3) take a supply home and dose themselves. The name for the treatment program was Body And Soul & Earth (BASE) Restoration.

The next Tid-Bits of Health article announced the program and invited people to try the products for 10 days. BASE Restoration was launched on February 20, 2017. It didn't take long for over 150 people to have gone through the program. Almost everyone chose multiple 10 day programs because they received such good results.

Other communities began asking for a BASE Restoration program. The scientist said this is how medicine will be practiced in the future.

The cost of the 10-Day program is made affordable through fundraisers and donations to the Altruistic United Humanity Association, a 501 (C) 3. This association is dedicated to the research, education, and treatment of these all-herbal dietary supplements.

A doctor who treated football players in the NFL stopped in one day and said, "People receive better treatment here than they do at their doctor's offices." It's the greatest thing in the world to see people feel better, have more natural energy, be free of depression, blood sugar problems, pain, headaches, and foggy thinking, etc.

On one hand, the accident was a major setback for me. On the other hand, it caused me to let go of the thoughts and feelings that were interfering with the business's progress. It made me submit to the guidance that propels one toward prosperity and greatness. My personal experience with the product line from Golden Sunrise Nutraceutical gave me the confidence I needed to teach the people in my community to "prosper and be in health even as their soul prospers."

A friend asked me, "Do you have difficulty going past the crumpled guard rail on the road every day?"

I said, "No. I just raise my hand and say, 'Thank you for my life. Thank you for all the Prayer Warriors around the world who dropped to their knees when they heard the news. Thank you for the lessons. And thank You, Choreographer-of-Coincidences, for carrying me through it all, for putting me back on my feet again, for keeping my friends close, and igniting my passion for a healthy community.'"

Like a pebble shot from a slingshot, my passion, now, lies between my trust in the Choreographer-of-Coincidences and my submission to His guidance that I feel in my gut. Now, when my decisions and ideas don't pan out the way I think they should, I trust that the Choreographer-of-Coincidences is working out His perfect plan instead of mine. I submit to Him, let go of mine, and let him launch me in the direction that I was meant to go. Where I can touch as many lives as possible and help "make the sorrowing glad."

***

*Sylvia is a natural-born teacher who puts her lessons into analogies to help her students grasp the lessons more completely. She completed her Licensed Practical Nurse's training at Walla Walla Community College then received her Bachelor's degree from Walla Walla College. She taught Physical Education on the college level then finished her Master's degree at Utah State University. She has held teaching positions from Junior High to College levels with many classes and programs in between. Her favorite private lesson was teaching a blind person to drive her Toyota pickup with a stick shift. Today, she focuses her attention on teaching people to take charge of their health at the cellular level, where it counts the most. She authored the **Body-Languages & Body-Money Manual,** which was used as one of the textbooks in her college health course for 15 years. Her love of nature, children, and backpacking culminate in the **Teddy Bear Adventure Series** of books for children. Sylvia became the Public Relations & Event Organizer for The Altruistic United Humanity Association, a 501 (c) (3), charitable organization that handles donations for Medical Treatment and Medical Research. She also developed the Body And Soul & Earth (BASE) Restoration treatment program for the Golden Sunrise Nutraceutical's product line.*

260

www.ingramcontent.com/pod-product-compliance
Lightning Source LLC
Chambersburg PA
CBHW031150270326
41931CB00006B/218